MATTHE

MATTHEW ARNOLD

Selected Poems

*Edited with an Introduction
by Keith Silver*

Fyfield Books

First published in 1994 by
Carcanet Press Limited
208-212 Corn Exchange Buildings
Manchester M4 3BQ

A CIP catalogue record for this book
is available from the British Library.
ISBN 1 85754 018 2

The publisher acknowledges financial assistance
from the Arts Council of Great Britain

Set in 10pt Palatino by Bryan Williamson, Frome
Printed and bound in England by SRP Ltd, Exeter

Contents

Introduction

On 11 August 1820 Thomas Arnold of Oriel College, Oxford was married to Mary Penrose. Having lost his bachelor status, Arnold was obliged to surrender his fellowship, a course which cannot have been easy for this unusually earnest young man with academic ambitions. Faced with the prospect of making a living, he settled at Laleham-on-Thames in Middlesex where, together with his brother-in-law John Buckland, he founded a private tutorial establishment. It was not long before married life began to offer compensations; on Christmas Eve of 1822 Mary Arnold gave birth to a first son, Matthew. In good health, save for a slight limp for which specialists prescribed a cumbersome iron leg brace – thus occasioning the rather harsh nickname of 'Crab' or 'Crabby' – Matthew flourished with his father's career. When he began his education as a boarder with Buckland, nine years and five brothers and sisters later, Dr Arnold was already installed as the controversial new headmaster of Rugby.

After a three-year spell under the tutelage of Herbert Hill, son-in-law to the Poet Laureate Robert Southey, Matthew and his brother Tom were despatched to their father's old school, Winchester College. Evidently things had declined since Dr Arnold's day. Not long after his thirteen-year-old son had nonchalantly described his tasks in the Winchester fifth form as 'light and easy', both boys were transferred to Arnoldian Rugby. Here, under a severe regime which stressed the primacy of moral character and religious instruction over academic attainment, Matthew followed such distinguished pupils as Arthur Penrhyn Stanley and Thomas Hughes. It is a measure of Dr Arnold's personal magnetism that both Stanley and Hughes later paid him literary tribute: an earnest first biography, *The Life and Correspondence of Thomas Arnold* and the affectionate memoir-as-novel, *Tom Brown's School Days*, did much to establish the headmaster's fearsome reputation. At the same time his vision of a Christian education was given currency by those of his pupils who, following his example to the utmost, became headmasters themselves.

The model pupil of the generation immediately prior to Matthew's had been the young Arthur Hugh Clough. While Matthew would have known Clough as one of his father's favourite boys, the pair did not become intimate until they encountered one another again at Oxford. A four-year age gap does not seem to have prevented their relationship from being conducted on equal terms. Besides Dr Arnold's paternal influence and bracing Rugby education, the two shared an interest in poetry and even a personal mythology, famously recalled in Arnold's 'The Scholar Gipsy' and 'Thyrsis'. This centred upon a story recounted in Joseph Glanvil's *The Vanity of Dogmatizing* (1661), which described how a promising student abandoned his books to seek the natural wisdom of the gipsies. Some two hundred years later Arnold and Clough would amuse themselves by imagining this wraith-like figure still shyly at large in the Oxfordshire countryside, miraculously preserved from the complexities of modern life. 'Thyrsis', Arnold's elegy for Clough, transforms this playful faith into a fraternal bond and a rare declaration of hope.

In later life this arcadian harmony was to prove as elusive as its magical representative. As time passed, each friend developed an intellectual impatience with the other's pursuit of the common vocation. Arnold, seeking something of the gipsy scholar's immunity, urged Clough to become detached by cultivating the 'Indian virtue'. Clough, on the other hand, advocated a zealous engagement with the world and took ideas seriously in a way which recalled Dr Arnold's fervour. Young Arnold preferred wandering in the Cumnor hills to the religious debates engendered by the Oxford Movement. While he could freely admire the brilliance of Newman's oratory, he remained blissfully aloof from those questions concerning the viability of the Thirty-Nine Articles which had once vexed his father. After a good deal of procrastination, Clough's doubts eventually lead him to resign his fellowship of Oriel, less in the name of tractarianism or rationalism than of intellectual freedom.

Arnold might have appreciated the grandeur of this gesture without really comprehending its moral imperatives. While he always remained subtly alive to generalized disharmonies –

coming to recognize straightforward choices between belief or nihilism, culture or anarchy – Clough agonized over doctrinal niceties. This fundamental difference in outlook goes some way towards explaining the disappointment each felt with the other's verse: 'his piping took a troubled sound' is the best that Arnold can say in the coded pastoral retrospect of 'Thyrsis'. If Clough was disappointed with Arnold, he reserved his most vehement reproaches for himself, always conscious of not having lived up to the promise of his prize-winning school years. After taking a second at Balliol College in 1841, he told Dr Arnold in characteristically uncompromising terms 'I have failed.'

Clough made several visits to Fox How, the Arnolds' Lake District holiday home near Ambleside. Full of unexpected talent, he distinguished himself as a fine swimmer – although there was not always time for such relaxation. Clough often felt obliged to work vigorously in order to set an example to his errant friend. In July 1844, when Matthew was supposed to be reading for his degree, Clough was writing anguished letters complaining that: 'Matt has gone out fishing when he ought properly to have been working.' Matt might have gained a more sympathetic response from his father's neighbour and walking companion, William Wordsworth. He certainly spent some edifying hours in the company of the ageing poet when his examinations were over. According to Mary Arnold, Wordsworth took Matthew under his 'special protection', both being 'second class men'.

Neither his indifferent degree, a penchant for fishing, nor a youthful reputation as a dilettante prevented Matthew from surprising his family by following in his father's footsteps to become a Fellow of Oriel in 1845. The Arnolds received another shock four years later, when a first collection of verse, *The Strayed Reveller and Other Poems* (1849), displayed an unsuspected preoccupation with moral issues. Consisting of a series of occasional sonnets and highly-coloured assays in the fashionable exotic mode – a superior example is 'The Sick King of Bokhara' – the volume also included Arnold's haunting nursery poem 'The Forsaken Merman' and the remarkably assured title piece, an early excursion into classical themes. The less luxuriant, more overtly 'philosophical'

9

writing is strongly marked by the presence of Wordsworth. Another well-known poem, 'Shakespeare', perhaps the definitive example of Victorian bardolatry, couches itself in distinctly Wordsworthian terms; the 'unguessed at' peasant poet, 'self-schooled, self-scanned', inspired directly by nature.

The complex literary relationship between Arnold and Wordsworth emerges powerfully in 'Resignation – to Fausta', the meditative *tour de force* which closes the book. In many ways this poem constitutes a self-conscious attempt on Arnold's part to distinguish himself from his mentor and, more particularly, from the evocation of a Nature which leads unproblematically 'from joy to joy'. These words come from Wordsworth's 'Tintern Abbey', which forms the model, or more accurately the foil, for Arnold's poem. Like Wordsworth, Arnold addresses his ruminations to a favourite sister on the occasion of a return to a familiar landscape. What he has to say, however, is a good deal less comforting: Fausta (the Goetherian pseudonym for Jane Arnold) must lower her expectations if she is to have any chance of happiness in a world characterized by the relentless amorality of natural forces. There may well be some quiet consolation in

> That life, whose dumb wish is not missed
> If birth proceeds, if things subsist;
> The life of plants, and stones, and rain ...

While Arnold struggles hard here to develop an independent voice, it is worth noticing that this is remarkably similar to the consolation that Wordsworth dourly offers himself in 'A slumber did my spirit seal', when imagining the dead Lucy 'Rolled round in earth's diurnal course,/ With rocks, and stones, and trees'. The point is that even at his most crushingly sceptical – in the dramatic poem 'Empedocles on Etna', which was to be the title piece of his next collection – Arnold does not abandon either Wordsworth's language or his basic premise. He forcefully differentiates himself, not through open disagreement, but by teasing out the blacker implications of his predecessor's pantheism.

> All things the world which fill
> Of but one stuff are spun,

>   That we who rail are still,
>   With what we rail at, one;
>   One with the o'erlabour'd Power that through the breadth
>   and length
>
>   Of earth, and air, and sea,
>   In men, and plants, and stones,
>   Hath toil perpetually,
>   And travails, pants, and moans;
>   Fain would do all things well, but sometimes fails in strength.
>   (I.ii. 287-96)

For Arnold, Nature is a tyrant as well as an enlightened despot.
When he encountered the view expressed in Coleridge's 'Dejec-
tion', 'Oh lady! we receive but what we give/ And in our life alone
does Nature live,' he condemned what he took to be human arro-
gance:

>   But man has a thousand gifts
>   And the generous dreamer invests
>   The senseless world with them all.
>   Nature is nothing: her charm
>   Lives in our eyes that can paint,
>   Lives in our hearts which can feel
>   'The Youth of Man' (32-7)

These lines are shot through with the existential hubris which
Arnold habitually attributed to the Utilitarians. Inevitably the
speaker soon becomes old and miserable and lives to regret his
naïve presumptions about human self-sufficiency. Even Words-
worth himself, suggests a companion piece, 'The Youth of
Nature', is not required to guarantee our joyful apprehension of
the landscapes he presented in his verse.

If the young Arnold had to wrestle with Wordsworth's legacy,
the influence of his father was incalculably more subtle and
oppressive. Dr Arnold had not lived to applaud the publication of
The Strayed Reveller. After his sudden death of heart disease in
1842, his presence had been reverently perpetuated by Mrs

11

Arnold at Fox How, which became what amounted to a family shrine. For Matthew the Doctor may have been almost as formidable dead as alive. Throughout his life the demands of family propriety and public duty strove with the need to be true to his own natural course of development. How far might Arnold have been attempting to subvert the achievements of his dead father – seemingly the epitome of human agency – when he stressed human inadequacy in the face of time and nature? There is evidence that, in order to preserve a sense of identity under Dr Arnold's intimidating shadow, he deliberately restrained or concealed his emotional responses. He later consciously accentuated them for the same reasons, adopting the manners and appearance of a Parisian dandy. Clough, in a more humorously censorious vein, described his painfully unmusical friend '...with a chanson of Béranger's on his lips – for the sake of French words almost conscious of tune: his carriage shows him in fancy parading the Rue de Rivoli; – and his hair is guiltless of English scissors...'. In the terminology of his two favourite English poets, this was a showy Byronic attack to compliment an introspective, Wordsworthian defence. A protectiveness, even a relish for secrecy informs the central idea of 'The Buried Life' (1852), that however many bogus selves circumstances may force us to assume, the life of our genuine self continues beneath, like the flow of a subterranean river. Arnold points to a hidden source, relentless as the natural world, but one which in our fallen condition we can only reach intermittently. There are various heroic antecedents for this: Shakespeare's Henry V who, 'like himself' assumes the port of Mars; Keats's vanquished Saturn, who laments the loss of 'my real self'; and Arnold's own Rustum – widely recognized by critics as an incarnation of Dr Arnold – whose arrogant boast of puissance is 'Am not I myself?' Wordsworth's reference in *The Prelude* to 'That calm existence which is mine when I am worthy of myself' comes closer to Arnold's meaning here, because the desired state of potency is a tranquil one and because the distance between it and a normal unexalted condition is freely acknowledged. The same discrepancy is apparent to Rustum, but that fierce, rhetorical 'Am not I myself?' makes for an edgy disclaimer.

Either way the 'real self' cannot be taken for granted, whether we fly up to it in a surge of inspiration, bully it into being with a fit of martial chest-beating, or, as Arnold does in 'The Buried Life', meditatively sink down below the flux of our daily concerns.

By the time Arnold came to write his major prose work *Culture and Anarchy* (published in 1869), an important ambiguity was beginning to emerge which would eventually draw him closer to Coleridge's position in 'Dejection'. Here he developed his famous concept of 'the best self', a practical amalgam of the finest qualities of a nation or an individual. Although the immediate goal of best selfhood is similar to that of 'The Buried Life', calm and a consequent integrity, Arnold is operating at yet another remove because unlike 'true' or 'genuine', 'best' implies an element of choice. We select the most propitious-looking persona from a number of possible selves. Ironically, this discretion, dismissed throughout the book as 'doing what one likes', is a part of the Anarchy to which Culture is offered as an antidote. The three-tier evolution through the self, the genuine self and the best self implicitly allies Arnold with Coleridge. This is not to say that he ever came to concede that 'the generous dreamer' really *does* invest the senseless world, any more than he would have agreed that the special generosity of a great poet like Wordsworth could alter forever our perceptions of his native lakes and mountains. But there is some incongruity in a position which holds, on the one hand, that it is vanity to suppose an individual to be capable of 're-creating' a landscape while, on the other, exhorting us to choose or create, through careful reading, our best self.

Something of this divided nature was perceived by Charlotte Brontë, who encountered 'Dr Arnold's young representative' in a London drawing-room, registering 'a real modesty ... under his assumed conceit'. Despite unlooked-for signs of maturity, Arnold remained restless. Following a spell as a temporary assistant master at Rugby, he had taken a steady job as Private Secretary to the Liberal peer Lord Landsdowne. In this sophisticated new environment he was able to indulge his enthusiasm for all things continental and more especially French. In the previous year he had spent eight months in France, visiting the scandalous authoress George Sand and renewing his admiration for the talents of the actress Rachel. In 1848 he embarked again, this time on a walking tour of Switzerland. That September the following lines were despatched to Clough: 'Tomorrow I will pass the Gemmi and get to Thun: linger one day for the sake of the blue eyes of one of its inmates, and then proceed by slow stages down the Rhine...'

The blue eyes in question belonged to the woman Arnold later referred to as Marguerite. This name and a few other details – her French nationality, the lilac handkerchief binding her hair, a languid cheek suggesting that she may have been a convalescent taking the alpine air – are known to us only from what became the *Switzerland* cycle of lyrics and a handful of corroborative letters. There is no trace of letters passed between Arnold and Marguerite, although we know that their love affair was sustained over a year's difficult absence. The sequence opens with the scene-setting poem 'Meeting', which describes the couple's joyful reunion at Thun the following September. Although purporting to immediacy ('Again I see my bliss at hand') the first lines read rather like old news necessarily retold; there is an incongruous impatience mingled with weariness masking the approach of this 'bliss'. Real urgency does not begin to be felt until the penultimate stanza introduces a hopeless sense of the impossibility of it all, as though decreed by some malevolent deity: 'I hear a God's tremendous voice,/ Be counselled and retire'. This same notion of a mysterious divine impediment occurs again, with richer implications, in the magnificent final lines of 'To Marguerite – Continued':

> Who ordered, that their longing's fire
> Should be, as soon as kindled, cooled?
> Who renders vain their deep desire? –
> A God, a God their severance ruled!
> And bade betwixt their shores to be
> The unplumbed, salt, estranging sea.

The power of the sequence, no matter how many times Arnold –

sensitive to his past – later rearranged it, lies in its inevitability, a painful realization that history has somehow already been accomplished. The knowledge of cooling love has been tragically present all along, and the lines in 'A Farewell' which make this explicit – 'Thy hand lay languidly in mine/ Thy cheek was grave, thy speech grew rare' – are merely an articulation of what is already felt. Arnold, like anyone else, found many ways of attempting to account for the failure of his relationship and in one respect *Switzerland* is an exorcism of these competing scenarios: blaming himself, he cites a lack of masculine steadfastness, his own feminine susceptibility to those vacillating passions women naturally seek refuge from in men. More convincing to the modern reader are the pitiful strictures about 'our different past'; Marguerite, it seems, had been held by other arms. Perhaps this was more than a puritanical streak in Arnold – the trait which perhaps drew him to the Alps in the first place – was able to endure. Certainly he consoled himself with visions of the gloomy mountain retirement of Senancour's Obermann; the salute to the forgotten French sage, 'Stanzas in Memory of the Author of Obermann' also dates from this visit. But the detachment which Arnold had always cultivated seemed momentarily to have deserted him. Clough may well have wondered what had come over his old friend when he was informed 'I am here in a curious and not altogether comfortable state.'

While *Switzerland* represents Arnold at his most Romantic, it is also symptomatic, like 'Resignation', of a deliberate turning away from those extremes of feeling which he remained content to enjoy at second-hand via an enthusiastic reading of Byron. These poems, rather than enacting a desperate rebellion against tyrannical gods, embody a sad capitulation to them; Arnold *is* counselled and he *does* retire. Similarly he emerges not so much as a poet anxious to preempt his own death as one prematurely arrived at middle age.

If we sometimes speak of people as having been born middle-aged, Arnold, the self-conscious product of a middle-aged civilization, elevates this state to the condition of prophesy. In the early meditation 'A Gipsy Child by the Sea Shore', the infant protagonist is mysteriously able to 'foreknow suffering', a capacity with which Arnold felt powerful affinities. By the time he published his second volume, *Empedocles on Etna and Other Poems* (1852), he had abandoned the idealization of childhood and replaced it with an idealization of youth; his equivalents to Wordsworth's Idiot Boy or the child-poet of the Immortality Ode became figures such as Callicles in 'Empedocles on Etna' and later the Scholar Gipsy and Thyrsis. Behind these visions of innocence there is a distinctive negative precociousness, not so much an advance beyond childhood as a contraction of life as a whole. Arnold had already lectured Fausta on the strange gift of the poet, 'Whose natural insight can discern/ What through experience others learn'; now he proved that he could take the hint offered him by his own instincts.

It is as though the break with Marguerite gave all the prescient scepticism which had haunted Arnold's youth its simultaneous, overwhelming confirmation. He wrote to Clough in 1849, 'we know beforehand all they (women) can teach us: yet we are obliged to learn it directly from them'. The last poem of the Swiss sequence, 'On the Terrace at Berne', composed some ten years later, is a wistful evocation of Marguerite and what might have become of her. Arnold's restless creative energy, born of disappointed love, is balanced by a post-Romantic sensibility that can 'foreknow suffering': 'I knew it when my life was young/ I feel it still, now youth is o'er'.

Perhaps more important than what Arnold actually 'knows' is the characteristic composure he gains from feeling that he knows. He urges Fausta in 'Resignation' not to seek to understand too much and yet the dangerous presumption is that his own knowledge, although restricted in scope, can be timeless in its validity. This qualified sense of limitation is succinctly expressed in the same poem in the formula 'not deep the poet sees but wide.' We find Arnold driving the point home to Clough in a letter dated February 1849:

I often think that...a slight gift of poetical expression...is overlaid and crushed in a profound thinker...The trying to go into the bottom of an object instead of grouping objects is as fatal to the sensuousness of poetry as the mere painting...is to its airy and rapidly moving life.

Besides the obvious rift between thought and feeling, this passage serves amply to demonstrate the generalizing character of Arnold's mind. He was not a poet (or critic) who could meticulously trace distress to its sources, as some commentators have upheld; in fact Arnold often exploits the very indefinability of these sources for aesthetic effect. Perhaps the central Arnoldian poetic emotion is bafflement, Keats's negative capability given a modern twist. Besides the tactic of deifying incomprehension in *Switzerland* there are, throughout Arnold's verse, repeated references to some ultimate, unknowable flaw: 'The something that infects the world' ('Resignation'); 'something has impaired thy spirit's strength/ And dried its self-sufficing font of joy' ('Empedocles on Etna'); 'a something in this breast/ To which thy light words bring no rest' ('The Buried Life'). In 'A Farewell', Arnold pardons Marguerite for failing to love one whose heart contains 'something in its depths.../ Too strange, too restless, too untamed.' There is no progress towards identifying the sources of distress but a growing assurance in uttering unpalatable truths.

If *Switzerland* had been a novel rather than the work of an intellectual poet, the sentimental Victorian public might well have demanded a more optimistic conclusion, just as Dickens provided an alternative happy ending to *Great Expectations*. In a sense this is what happened anyway. Strewn through the beginning of Arnold's 1852 volume were the poems that would eventually comprise a second sequence, 'Faded Leaves', an account of the not exactly trouble-free courtship of Frances Lucy Wightman, the daughter of a prominent judge. The title is unfortunate, suggesting a paler version of the earlier affair, and it is difficult when viewing the poems as a sequence to avoid the conclusion that they were arranged thus in an effort to balance the record for posterity. Arnold had already hastily amended the refrain of the preface poem to *Switzerland*, 'A Memory Picture', from 'Ere the parting kiss be dry' to the safer 'Ere the parting hour go by', and later told his children that his relationship with Marguerite only ever existed as a literary conceit. Perhaps that was half-true. In any case this was only tactful since, after Arnold had managed to convince Justice Wightman that he would be able to support a wife – thanks to the timely intervention of Lord Landsdowne who appointed him Inspector of Schools – he and Frances Lucy were married on 10 June 1851. If readers still need consolation, there is the famous lyric which Arnold probably wrote before the couple's departure on their delayed continental honeymoon, 'Dover Beach'.

'Dover Beach' was in several ways a watershed poem for Arnold. At the beginning of his marriage he looks across the 'unplumbed, salt, estranging sea' towards France and discovers in the retreating tide an intimation of desolate anarchy. Dealing with a characteristically undefined and undefinable sense of loss, the poem rejects melancholy indulgence to conclude with a calmly unambiguous expression of despair, anticipating the bare didactic lyrics – 'Growing Old', 'The Progress of Poesy' – which were to form the coda of his poetic career in 1867. The sea is more frankly employed as a metaphor even than in 'To Marguerite – Continued', displaying a shift away from Wordsworthian Nature, subsumed beautifully by abstract thought. The great exclamation, 'Love, let us be true to one another' has more desperation about it than tenderness. At the same time what Kenneth Allott describes as 'the one dubiously "poetical" line in the poem', the visually problematic, rhythmically anomalous 'folds of a bright girdle furled', points to a sort of defensive contraction, a moment of rhythmical conservatism. Arnold, alongside Whitman, was the greatest practitioner of free verse in the nineteenth century, but a comparison of his typically short lines with Whitman's typically long ones suggests a lack of confidence in the face of new freedoms. The metre here closes thankfully around the irrefutably musical half-rhyme.

In fact the tide was coming in for Arnold. Marriage had imposed a new set of obligations which, in the light of his father-in-law's

18

initial scruples, must have seemed all the more intractable. The School Inspector's job meant a reasonable income but also long hours and a great deal of travelling, which did little for the intense concentration which Arnold's processes of verse composition demanded. He would rise early to work in hotel bedrooms in the thriving industrial cities of Victorian England – Birmingham, Manchester, Sheffield, Leeds, Liverpool – places where contemporary thinkers, aware of the power of a rising working class, would occasionally venture to address the new mechanics institutes; where Arnold himself once told a crowd, 'you must try to be patient'. The new conditions of his life, with their demands for a quicker, more practical mode of thought, lent themselves to the preparation of public speeches and prose rather than poetry. Among Arnold's first important prose works were his professional treatises on education – ground-breaking writings like *The Popular Education of France* and *A French Eton* which drew upon direct knowledge of French, Italian, German and Swiss models gained during extensive travels as Foreign Assistant Commissioner to the Education Commission in 1859. These reports constitute a calculated assault on that national educational complacency which Dr Arnold had almost come to symbolize, and in this respect probably represent Arnold's most successful act of rebellion.

The School Inspector's job was to occupy Arnold until his retirement in 1886, save for a ten-year interlude as Oxford Professor of Poetry, a position he treated with an unprecedented seriousness, becoming the first incumbent to lecture in English. During this time he consolidated a reputation which had slowly grown through the publication of *Empedocles on Etna and Other Poems* and, crucially, *Poems, A New Edition* (1853). From this point onwards Arnold's book of poems became a protean, ongoing concern – a little like Whitman's *Leaves of Grass* on the other side of the Atlantic. New pieces were added to the existing volume, most notably the pastoral elegies 'The Scholar Gipsy' and 'Thyrsis', and 'Sohrab and Rustum', which ushered in an interest in epic forms. Meanwhile the development of Arnold's critical faculties sometimes lead to the removal of earlier work, the most significant casualty being 'Empedocles on Etna', which was not reinstated until championed by Browning in 1867. Although Arnold celebrated the end of his tenure at Oxford with a new edition, the poet was already half-eclipsed by the critic. In 1853 and 1854 he wrote elaborate prefaces explaining the aims behind his published verse, at around the same time beginning to produce poems like 'Balder Dead' and the ill-conceived 'Merope' with the express intention of embodying the precepts of this manifesto. The change of priorities is evident.

The hero of Arnold's early criticism is Homer, whom he regarded, like many twentieth century authors, as a symbol of literary integration. The Greek epics could provide a panacea for the isolated, self-questioning Romantic artist because they were seen to carry the authority of a whole society. Accordingly, a preoccupation of his later verse is an oblique attempt to rival the Homeric cultural synthesis. Goethe, a potential modern Homer, is, he intimates, compelled to become a sort of one man culture, drawing upon the German critical tradition and his own great intellectual resources in the absence of an authentic 'national glow'. It is the task of criticism to create an artificial context for such a disowned talent. A modern epic would require a strenuous apprenticeship along the lines of Coleridge's projected twenty years, or Wordsworth's autobiographical procrastination in *The Prelude*. The raw materials of Arnold's own culture building enterprise, at first as much an artistic problem as a social one, are as diverse and eclectic as those outlined in the opening section of that poem. Wordsworth's wide-ranging catalogue of rejected subjects – Spenserian chivalry, abstract philosophy, Scandinavian folklore – is allied to Arnold's affinities with Joubert, Senancour or the actress Rachel (and ultimately to the notes at the end of *The Waste Land*) by a charismatic idiosyncrasy. These are all strongly personal 'cultures' and it is clear that value is awarded in a way which has a direct bearing on each writer's particular imaginative needs. In Joubert and Senancour and Rachel, and also in Wordsworth and Goethe, are the beginnings of the culture of *Culture and Anarchy*, but it is the opposite of a socially unifying force. Like the modernists after him, the more comprehensively Arnold sought to compensate for his artistic isolation, the more esoteric he risked becoming.

Although not exactly Arnold's epic, *Culture and Anarchy*, which appeared in 1869, was his most ambitious attempt at a grand reconciliation. Strewn with infectious catch-phrases – 'doing as one likes', 'Sweetness and light', 'high seriousness', 'Hebraism and Helenism' – and the neat delineation of the English social structure into Barbarians, Philistines and Populace, it immediately established Arnold as a popular sage, apparently with the endorsement of the young Princess Alice, who was among its most enthusiastic readers. Although eventually outsold by *Literature and Dogma* (1873), Arnold's blockbusting attempt to apply the principles of literary criticism to the Bible and thereby save Christianity from rationalism, nothing he ever did quite caught the public imagination in the same way.

This says something important about Arnold's capacity to create binding myths. His attempt to unite the whole of English society is not too dissimilar from his Arcadian rapprochement with Clough in 'Thyrsis', or the thinking which underlay his late excursions into the Homeric 'Grand Style'. Exotic as the ancient Persian setting of 'Sohrab and Rustum' or the legendary Norse twilight of 'Balder Dead' might seem, they did not exclusively represent an attempt to withdraw into a more congenial world. Arnold was always less well equipped – financially and perhaps imaginatively – than either Tennyson or Browning to stage this kind of retreat. For this very reason he may, as he once claimed, stand closer to 'the main line of modern development' than either. For Arnold mythology became less a means of transcendence or escape than a formulation of humanistic values to set against the Victorian malaise. His melancholy was always a different thing from Tennyson's dreaminess, his passivity of a stoical nature which was intimately related to assertive didacticism.

The increasingly confident public voice of Arnold's later years reflected harsh experience. In 1868, the year after the end of his professorship, he was stunned by the deaths of his infant son

Basil and of his eldest son Thomas, then at Harrow. The only elegies that Arnold had left in him now were for family pets. This was a natural end to his poetic career rather than an evasion, another hard truth had to be accepted. In spite, or perhaps because of his prescience, Arnold the poet had lived and died young.

Select Bibliography

The most comprehensive general edition of Arnold's poems currently available is *Arnold – The Complete Poems* (ed. Kenneth Allott, Longman, 1965. Second Edition ed. Miriam Allott, Longman, 1979). Exhaustively annotated, this contains several valuable appendices, including examples of Arnold's juvenilia and details of the contents of the original volumes. The prose is less well served. *Matthew Arnold, Selected Prose* (ed. P.J. Keating, Penguin, 1970) is widely available and provides a useful introduction to the range of Arnold's literary and social criticism. John Dover Wilson's informative edition of *Culture and Anarchy* (1935) has been issued in paperback by Cambridge University Press, and a new selection of the correspondence, *Selected Letters of Matthew Arnold* (ed. Clinton Machann and Forest D. Burt, Macmillan) appeared in 1993. The definitive editions here are *The Complete Prose Works of Matthew Arnold* (11 vols, ed. R.H. Super, 1960-1977) and *Letters of Matthew Arnold, 1848-1888* (2 vols, ed. G.W.E. Russell, 1895).

Perhaps the most influential single critical work on Arnold, Lionel Trilling's *Matthew Arnold* (Columbia University Press, 1939) is now out of print, but worth pursuing at well-stocked libraries. So are *The Poetry of Matthew Arnold, A Commentary* by C.B. Tinker and H.F. Lowry (Oxford University Press, 1940) and *Matthew Arnold and English Romanticism*, by D.G. James (Oxford University Press, 1961). F.R. Leavis's negative verdict on Arnold appears in *Revaluation* (Chatto & Windus, 1936). Raymond Williams's *Culture and Society 1780-1950* (Chatto & Windus, 1958) provides an absorbing, guardedly sympathetic appraisal of Arnold's social thought.

Shakespeare

Others abide our question. Thou art free.
We ask and ask – Thou smilest and art still,
Out-topping knowledge. For the loftiest hill,
Who to the stars uncrowns his majesty,

Planting his steadfast footsteps in the sea,
Making the heaven of heavens his dwelling-place,
Spares but the cloudy border of his base
To the foiled searching of mortality;

And thou, who didst the stars and sunbeams know,
Self-schooled, self-scanned, self-honoured, self-secure,
Didst tread on earth unguessed at. – Better so!

All pains the immortal spirit must endure,
All weakness which impairs, all griefs which bow,
Find their sole speech in that victorious brow.

The Sick King in Bokhara

Hussein

O most just Vizier, send away
The cloth-merchants, and let them be,
Them and their dues, this day! the King
Is ill at ease, and calls for thee.

The Vizier

O merchants, tarry yet a day
Here in Bokhara! but at noon,
To-morrow, come, and ye shall pay
Each fortieth web of cloth to me,
As the law is, and go your way.

25

O Hussein, lead me to the King!   10
Thou teller of sweet tales, thine own,
Ferdousi's, and the others', lead!
How is it with my lord?

Hussein

Alone,
Ever since prayer-time, he doth wait,
O Vizier! without lying down,
In the great window of the gate,
Looking into the Registàn,
Where through the sellers' booths the slaves
Are this way bringing the dead man. –   20
O Vizier, here is the King's door!

The King

O Vizier, I may bury him?

The Vizier

O King, thou know'st, I have been sick
These many days, and heard no thing
(For Allah shut my ears and mind),
Not even what thou dost, O King!
Wherefore, that I may counsel thee,
Let Hussein, if thou wilt, make haste
To speak in order what hath chanced.

The King

O Vizier, be it as thou say'st!   30

Hussein

Three days since, at the time of prayer
A certain Moollah, with his robe
All rent, and dust upon his hair,
Watched my lord's coming forth, and pushed
The golden mace-bearers aside,
And fell at the King's feet, and cried:

'Justice, O King, and on myself!
On this great sinner, who did break
The law, and by the law must die!
Vengeance, O King!'

           But the King spake: 40
'What fool is this, that hurts our ears
With folly? or what drunken slave?
My guards, what, prick him with your spears!
Prick me the fellow from the path!'
As the King said, so it was done,
And to the mosque my lord passed on.
But on the morrow, when the King
Went forth again, the holy book
Carried before him, as is right,
And through the square his way he took;   50
My man comes running, flecked with blood
From yesterday, and falling down
Cries out most earnestly, 'O King,
My lord, O King, do right, I pray!

'How canst thou, ere thou hear, discern
If I speak folly? but a king,
Whether a thing be great or small,
Like Allah, hears and judges all.

'Wherefore hear thou! Thou know'st, how fierce
In these last days the sun hath burned;   60
That the green water in the tanks
Is to a putrid puddle turned;
And the canal, which from the stream
Of Samarcand is brought this way,
Wastes, and runs thinner every day.

'Now I at nightfall had gone forth
Alone, and in a darksome place
Under some mulberry-trees I found
A little pool; and in short space,

With all the water that was there   70
I filled my pitcher, and stole home
Unseen; and having drink to spare,
I hid the can behind the door,
And went up on the roof to sleep.

'But in the night, which was with wind
And burning dust, again I creep
Down, having fever, for a drink.

'Now meanwhile had my brethren found
The water-pitcher, where it stood
Behind the door upon the ground,   80
And called my mother; and they all,
As they were thirsty, and the night
Most sultry, drained the pitcher there;
That they sate with it, in my sight,
Their lips still wet, when I came down.

'Now mark! I, being fevered, sick
(Most unblest also), at that sight
Brake forth, and cursed them – dost thou hear?
One was my mother – Now, do right!'
But my lord mused a space, and said: 90
'Send him away, Sirs, and make on!
It is some madman!' the King said.
As the King bade, so was it done.

The morrow, at the self-same hour,
In the King's path, behold, the man,
Not kneeling, sternly fixed! he stood
Right opposite, and thus began,

Frowning grim down: 'Thou wicked King,
Most deaf where thou shouldst most give ear!
What, must I howl in the next world,   100
Because thou wilt not listen here?

'What, wilt thou pray, and get thee grace,
And all grace shall to me be grudged?
Nay but, I swear, from this thy path
I will not stir till I be judged!'

Then they who stood about the King
Drew close together and conferred;
Till that the King stood forth and said:
'Before the priests thou shalt be heard.'

But when the Ulemas were met,   110
And the thing heard, they doubted not;
But sentenced him, as the law is,
To die by stoning on the spot.

Now the King charged us secretly:
'Stoned must he be, the law stands so.
Yet, if he seek to fly, give way;
Hinder him not, but let him go.'

So saying, the King took a stone,
And cast it softly; – but the man,
With a great joy upon his face,   120
Kneeled down, and cried not, neither ran.

So they, whose lot it was, cast stones,
That they flew thick and bruised him sore.
But he praised Allah with loud voice,
And remained kneeling as before.

My lord had covered up his face;
But when one told him, 'He is dead,'
Turning him quickly to go in,
'Bring thou to me his corpse,' he said.

And truly, while I speak, O King,   130
I hear the bearers on the stair;

Wilt thou they straightway bring him in?
– Ho! enter ye who tarry there!

The Vizier

O King, in this I praise thee not!
Now must I call thy grief not wise.
Is he thy friend, or of thy blood,
To find such favour in thine eyes?

Nay, were he thine own mother's son,
Still, thou art king, and the law stands.
It were not meet the balance swerved,   140
The sword were broken in thy hands.

But being nothing, as he is,
Why for no cause make sad thy face?
Lo, I am old! three kings, ere thee,
Have I seen reigning in this place.

But who, through all this length of time,
Could bear the burden of his years,
If he for strangers pained his heart
Not less than those who merit tears?

Fathers we *must* have, wife and child,   150
And grievous is the grief for these;
This pain alone, which *must* be borne,
Makes the head white, and bows the knees.

But other loads than this his own
One man is not well made to bear.
Besides, to each are his own friends,
To mourn with him, and show him care.

Look, this is but one single place,
Though it be great; all the earth round,
If a man bear to have it so,   160
Things which might vex him shall be found.

Upon the Russian frontier, where
The watchers of two armies stand
Near one another, many a man,
Seeking a prey unto his hand,

Hath snatched a little fair-haired slave;
They snatch also, towards Mervè,
The Shiah dogs, who pasture sheep,
And up from thence to Orgunjè.

And these all, labouring for a lord,   170
Eat not the fruit of their own hands;
Which is the heaviest of all plagues,
To that man's mind, who understands.

The kaffirs also (whom God curse!)
Vex one another, night and day;
There are the lepers, and all sick;
There are the poor, who faint alway.

All these have sorrow, and keep still,
Whilst other men make cheer, and sing.
Wilt thou have pity on all these?   180
No, nor on this dead dog, O King!

The King

O Vizier, thou art old, I young!
Clear in these things I cannot see.
My head is burning, and a heat
Is in my skin which angers me.

But hear ye this, ye sons of men!
They that bear rule, and are obeyed,
Unto a rule more strong than theirs
Are in their turn obedient made.

31

In vain therefore, with wistful eyes   190
Gazing up hither, the poor man,
Who loiters by the high-heaped booths,
Below there, in the Registàn,

Says: 'Happy he, who lodges there!
With silken raiment, store of rice,
And for this drought, all kinds of fruits,
Grape-syrup, squares of coloured ice,

'With cherries served in drifts of snow.'
In vain hath a king power to build
Houses, arcades, enamelled mosques;   200
And to make orchard-closes, filled

With curious fruit-trees brought from far;
With cisterns for the winter-rain,
And, in the desert, spacious inns
In divers places – if that pain

Is not more lightened, which he feels,
If his will be not satisfied;
And that it be not, from all time
The law is planted, to abide.

Thou wast a sinner, thou poor man!   210
Thou wast athirst; and didst not see,
That, though we take what we desire,
We must not snatch it eagerly.

And I have meat and drink at will,
And rooms of treasures, not a few.
But I am sick, nor heed I these;
And what I would, I cannot do.

Even the great honour which I have,
When I am dead, will soon grow still;

So have I neither joy, nor fame. 220
But what I can do, that I will.

I have a fretted brick-work tomb
Upon a hill on the right hand,
Hard by a close of apricots,
Upon the road of Samarcand;

Thither, O Vizier, will I bear
This man my pity could not save,
And, plucking up the marble flags,
There lay his body in my grave.

Bring water, nard, and linen rolls! 230
Wash off all blood, set smooth each limb!
Then say: 'He was not wholly vile,
Because a king shall bury him.'

Resignation

To Fausta

To die be given us, or attain!
Fierce work it were, to do again.
So pilgrims, bound for Mecca, prayed
At burning noon; so warriors said,
Scarfed with the cross, who watched the miles
Of dust which wreathed their struggling files
Down Lydian mountains; so, when snows
Round Alpine summits, eddying, rose,
The Goth, bound Rome-wards; so the Hun,
Crouched on his saddle, while the sun 10
Went lurid down o'er flooded plains
Through which the groaning Danube strains

33

To the drear Euxine; so pray all,
Whom labours, self-ordained, enthrall;
Because they to themselves propose
On this side the all-common close
A goal which, gained, may give repose.
So pray they; and to stand again
Where they stood once, to them were pain;
Pain to thread back and to renew   20
Past straits, and currents long steered through.

But milder natures, and more free –
Whom an unblamed serenity
Hath freed from passions, and the state
Of struggle these necessitate;
Whom schooling of the stubborn mind
Hath made, or birth hath found, resigned –
These mourn not, that their goings pay
Obedience to the passing day.
These claim not every laughing Hour   30
For handmaid to their striding power;
Each in her turn, with torch upreared,
To await their march; and when appeared,
Through the cold gloom, with measured race,
To usher for a destined space
(Her own sweet errands all forgone)
The too imperious traveller on.
These, Fausta, ask not this; nor thou,
Time's chafing prisoner, ask it now!

    We left, just ten years since, you say,   40
That wayside inn we left to-day.
Our jovial host, as forth we fare,
Shouts greeting from his easy chair.
High on a bank our leader stands,
Reviews and ranks his motley bands,
Makes clear our goal to every eye –
The valley's western boundary.

A gate swings to! our tide hath flowed
Already from the silent road.
The valley-pastures, one by one,   50
Are threaded, quiet in the sun;
And now beyond the rude stone bridge
Slopes gracious up the western ridge.
Its woody border, and the last
Of its dark upland farms is past –
Cool farms, with open-lying stores,
Under their burnished sycamores;
All past! and through the trees we glide,
Emerging on the green hill-side.
There climbing hangs, a far-seen sign,   60
Our wavering, many-coloured line;
There winds, upstreaming slowly still
Over the summit of the hill.
And now, in front, behold outspread
Those upper regions we must tread!
Mild hollows, and clear heathy swells,
The cheerful silence of the fells.

Some two hours' march with serious air,
Through the deep noontide heats we fare;
The red-grouse, springing at our sound,   70
Skims, now and then, the shining ground;
No life, save his and ours, intrudes
Upon these breathless solitudes.
O Joy! again the farms appear.
Cool shade is there, and rustic cheer;
There springs the brook will guide us down,
Bright comrade, to the noisy town.
Lingering, we follow down, we gain
The town, the highway, and the plain.
And many a mile of dusty way,   80
Parched and road-worn, we made that day;
But, Fausta, I remember well,
That as the balmy darkness fell

We bathed our hands with speechless glee,
That night, in the wide-glimmering sea.

Once more we tread this self-same road,
Fausta, which ten years since we trod;
Alone we tread it, you and I,
Ghosts of that boisterous company.
Here, where the brook shines, near its head,   90
In its clear, shallow, turf-fringed bed;
Here, whence the eye first sees, far down,
Capped with faint smoke, the noisy town;
Here sit we, and again unroll,
Though slowly, the familiar whole.
The solemn wastes of heathy hill
Sleep in the July sunshine still;
The self-same shadows now, as then,
Play through this grassy upland glen;
The loose dark stones on the green way   100
Lie strewn, it seems, where then they lay;
On this mild bank above the stream,
(You crush them!) the blue gentians gleam.
Still this wild brook, the rushes cool,
The sailing foam, the shining pool!
These are not changed; and we, you say,
Are scarce more changed, in truth, than they.

The gipsies, whom we met below,
They, too, have long roamed to and fro;
They ramble, leaving, where they pass,   110
Their fragments on the cumbered grass.
And often to some kindly place
Chance guides the migratory race,
Where, though long wanderings intervene,
They recognise a former scene.
The dingy tents are pitched; the fires
Give to the wind their wavering spires;
In dark knots crouch round the wild flame

Their children, as when first they came;
They see their shackled beasts again   120
Move, browsing, up the gray-walled lane.
Signs are not wanting, which might raise
The ghost in them of former days –
Signs are not wanting, if they would;
Suggestions to disquietude.
For them, for all, time's busy touch,
While it mends little, troubles much.
Their joints grow stiffer – but the year
Runs his old round of dubious cheer;
Chilly they grow – yet winds in March,   130
Still, sharp as ever, freeze and parch;
They must live still – and yet, God knows,
Crowded and keen the country grows;
It seems as if, in their decay,
The law grew stronger every day.
So might they reason, so compare,
Fausta, times past with times that are.
But no! – they rubbed through yesterday
In their hereditary way,
And they will rub through, if they can,   140
To-morrow on the self-same plan,
Till death arrive to supersede,
For them, vicissitude and need.

The poet, to whose mighty heart
Heaven doth a quicker pulse impart,
Subdues that energy to scan
Not his own course, but that of man.
Though he move mountains, though his day
Be passed on the proud heights of sway,
Though he hath loosed a thousand chains,   150
Though he hath borne immortal pains,
Action and suffering though he know –
He hath not lived, if he lives so.
He sees, in some great-historied land,

A ruler of the people stand,
Sees his strong thought in fiery flood
Roll through the heaving multitude;
Exults – yet for no moment's space
Envies the all-regarded place.
Beautiful eyes meet his – and he   160
Bears to admire uncravingly;
They pass – he, mingled with the crowd,
Is in their far-off triumphs proud.
From some high station he looks down,
At sunset, on a populous town;
Surveys each happy group which fleets,
Toil ended, through the shining streets,
Each with some errand of its own –
And does not say: *I am alone.*
He sees the gentle stir of birth   170
When morning purifies the earth;
He leans upon a gate and sees
The pastures, and the quiet trees.
Low, woody hill, with gracious bound,
Folds the still valley almost round;
The cuckoo, loud on some high lawn,
Is answered from the depth of dawn;
In the hedge straggling to the stream,
Pale, dew-drenched, half-shut roses gleam;
But, where the farther side slopes down,   180
He sees the drowsy new-waked clown
In his white quaint-embroidered frock
Make, whistling, tow'rd his mist-wreathed flock –
Slowly, behind his heavy tread,
The wet, flowered grass heaves up its head.
Leaned on his gate, he gazes – tears
Are in his eyes, and in his ears
The murmur of a thousand years.
Before him he sees life unroll,
A placid and continuous whole –   190
That general life, which does not cease,

Whose secret is not joy, but peace;
That life, whose dumb wish is not missed
If birth proceeds, if things subsist;
The life of plants, and stones, and rain,
The life he craves – if not in vain
Fate gave, what chance shall not control,
His sad lucidity of soul.

You listen – but that wandering smile,
Fausta, betrays you cold the while!   200
Your eyes pursue the bells of foam
Washed, eddying, from this bank, their home.
Those gipsies, so your thoughts I scan,
Are less, the poet more, than man.
They feel not, though they move and see;
Deeper the poet feels; but he
Breathes, when he will, immortal air,
Where Orpheus and where Homer are.
In the day's life, whose iron round
Hems us all in, he is not bound;   210
He leaves his kind, o'erleaps their pen,
And flees the common life of men.
He escapes thence, but we abide –
Not deep the poet sees, but wide.
The world in which we live and move
Outlasts aversion, outlasts love,
Outlasts each effort, interest, hope,
Remorse, grief, joy; and were the scope
Of these affections wider made,
Man still would see, and see dismayed,   220
Beyond his passion's widest range,
Far regions of eternal change.
Nay, and since death, which wipes out man,
Finds him with many an unsolved plan,
With much unknown, and much untried,
Wonder not dead, and thirst not dried,
Still gazing on the ever full

Eternal mundane spectacle –
This world in which we draw our breath,
In some sense, Fausta, outlasts death.   230

   Blame thou not, therefore, him who dares
Judge vain beforehand human cares;
Whose natural insight can discern
What through experience others learn;
Who needs not love and power, to know
Love transient, power an unreal show;
Who treads at ease life's uncheered ways –
Him blame not, Fausta, rather praise!
Rather thyself for some aim pray
Nobler than this, to fill the day;   240
Rather that heart, which burns in thee,
Ask, not to amuse, but to set free;
Be passionate hopes not ill resigned
For quiet, and a fearless mind.

And though fate grudge to thee and me
The poet's rapt security,
Yet they, believe me, who await
No gifts from chance, have conquered fate.
They, winning room to see and hear,
And to men's business not too near,   250
Through clouds of individual strife
Draw homeward to the general life.
Like leaves by suns not yet uncurled;
To the wise, foolish; to the world,
Weak; yet not weak, I might reply,
Not foolish, Fausta, in His eye,
To whom each moment in its race,
Crowd as we will its neutral space,
Is but a quiet watershed
Whence, equally, the seas of life and death are fed.   260

Enough, we live! and if a life,
With large results so little rife,
Though bearable, seem hardly worth
This pomp of worlds, this pain of birth;
Yet, Fausta, the mute turf we tread,
The solemn hills around us spread,
This stream which falls incessantly,
The strange-scrawled rocks, the lonely sky,
If I might lend their life a voice,
Seem to bear rather than rejoice.   270
And even could the intemperate prayer
Man iterates, while these forbear,
For movement, for an ampler sphere,
Pierce Fate's impenetrable ear;
Not milder is the general lot
Because our spirits have forgot,
In action's dizzying eddy whirled,
The something that infects the world.

The Forsaken Merman

Come, dear children, let us away;
Down and away below!
Now my brothers call from the bay,
Now the great winds shoreward blow,
Now the salt tides seaward flow;
Now the wild white horses play,
Champ and chafe and toss in the spray.
Children dear, let us away!
This way, this way!

Call her once before you go –   10
Call once yet!
In a voice that she will know:

41

'Margaret! Margaret!'
Children's voices should be dear
(Call once more) to a mother's ear;
Children's voices, wild with pain –
Surely she will come again!
Call her once and come away;
This way, this way!
'Mother dear, we cannot stay!   20
The wild white horses foam and fret.'
Margaret! Margaret!

Come, dear children, come away down;
Call no more!
One last look at the white-walled town,
And the little grey church on the windy shore,
Then come down!
She will not come though you call all day;
Come away, come away!

Children dear, was it yesterday   30
We heard the sweet bells over the bay?
In the caverns where we lay,
Through the surf and through the swell,
The far-off sound of a silver bell?
Sand-strewn caverns, cool and deep,
Where the winds are all asleep;
Where the spent lights quiver and gleam,
Where the salt weed sways in the stream,
Where the sea-beasts, ranged all round,
Feed in the ooze of their pasture-ground;   40
Where the sea-snakes coil and twine,
Dry their mail and bask in the brine;
Where great whales come sailing by,
Sail and sail, with unshut eye,
Round the world for ever and aye?
When did music come this way?
Children dear, was it yesterday?

42

Children dear, was it yesterday
(Call yet once) that she went away?
Once she sate with you and me,   50
On a red gold throne in the heart of the sea,
And the youngest sate on her knee.
She combed its bright hair, and she tended it well,
When down swung the sound of a far-off bell.
She sighed, she looked up through the clear green sea;
She said: 'I must go, for my kinsfolk pray
In the little grey church on the shore to-day.
'Twill be Easter-time in the world – ah me!
And I lose my poor soul, Merman! here with thee.'
I said: 'Go up, dear heart, through the waves;   60
Say thy prayer, and come back to the kind sea-caves!'
She smiled, she went up through the surf in the bay.
Children dear, was it yesterday?

    Children dear, were we long alone?
'The sea grows stormy, the little ones moan;
Long prayers,' I said, 'in the world they say;
Come!' I said; and we rose through the surf in the bay.
We went up the beach, by the sandy down
Where the sea-stocks bloom, to the white-walled town;
Through the narrow paved streets, where all was still,   70
To the little grey church on the windy hill.
From the church came a murmur of folk at their prayers,
But we stood without in the cold blowing airs.
We climbed on the graves, on the stones worn with rains,
And we gazed up the aisle through the small leaded
        panes.
She sate by the pillar; we saw her clear:
'Margaret, hist! come quick, we are here!
Dear heart,' I said, 'we are long alone;
The sea grows stormy, the little ones moan.'
But, ah, she gave me never a look,   80
For her eyes were sealed to the holy book!
Loud prays the priest; shut stands the door.

Come away, children, call no more!
Come away, come down, call no more!

   Down, down, down!
Down to the depths of the sea!
She sits at her wheel in the humming town,
Singing most joyfully.
Hark what she sings: 'O joy, O joy,
For the humming street, and the child with its toy!   90
For the priest, and the bell, and the holy well;
For the wheel where I spun,
And the blessed light of the sun!'
And so she sings her fill,
Singing most joyfully,
Till the spindle drops from her hand,
And the whizzing wheel stands still.
She steals to the window, and looks at the sand,
And over the sand at the sea;
And her eyes are set in a stare;   100
And anon there breaks a sigh,
And anon there drops a tear,
From a sorrow-clouded eye,
And a heart sorrow-laden,
A long, long sigh;
For the cold strange eyes of a little Mermaiden
And the gleam of her golden hair.

   Come away, away children:
Come children, come down!
The hoarse wind blows coldly;   110
Lights shine in the town.
She will start from her slumber
When gusts shake the door;
She will hear the winds howling,
Will hear the waves roar.
We shall see, while above us
The waves roar and whirl,

A ceiling of amber,
A pavement of pearl.
Singing: 'Here came a mortal,   120
But faithless was she!
And alone dwell for ever
The kings of the sea.'

But, children, at midnight,
When soft the winds blow,
When clear falls the moonlight,
When spring-tides are low;
When sweet airs come seaward
From heaths starred with broom,
And high rocks throw mildly   130
On the blanched sands a gloom;
Up the still, glistening beaches,
Up the creeks we will hie,
Over banks of bright seaweed
The ebb-tide leaves dry.
We will gaze, from the sand-hills,
At the white, sleeping town;
At the church on the hill-side –
And then come back down.
Singing: 'There dwells a loved one,   140
But cruel is she!
She left lonely for ever
The kings of the sea.'

A Memory Picture

Laugh, my friends, and without blame
Lightly quit what lightly came;
Rich to-morrow as to-day,
Spend as madly as you may!
I, with little land to stir,
Am the exacter labourer.
  Ere the parting hour go by,
  Quick, thy tablets, Memory!

Once I said: 'A face is gone
If too hotly mused upon;
And our best impressions are
Thost that do themselves repair.'
Many a face I so let flee,
Ah! is faded utterly.
  Ere the parting hour go by,
  Quick, thy tablets, Memory!

Marguerite says: 'As last year went,
So the coming year'll be spent;
Some day next year, I shall be,
Entering heedless, kissed by thee.'
Ah, I hope! – yet, once away,
What may chain us, who can say?
  Ere the parting hour go by,
  Quick, thy tablets, Memory!

Paint that lilac kerchief, bound
Her soft face, her hair around;
Tied under the archest chin
Mockery ever ambushed in.
Let the fluttering fringes streak
All her pale, sweet-rounded cheek.
  Ere the parting hour go by,
  Quick, thy tablets, Memory!

Paint that figure's pliant grace
As she tow'rd me leaned her face,
Half refused and half resigned,
Murmuring: 'Art thou still unkind?'
Many a broken promise then
Was new made – to break again.
  Ere the parting hour go by,
  Quick, thy tablets, Memory!   40

Paint those eyes, so blue, so kind,
Eager tell-tales of her mind;
Paint, with their impetuous stress
Of inquiring tenderness,
Those frank eyes, where deep I see
An angelic gravity.
  Ere the parting hour go by,
  Quick, thy tablets, Memory!

What, my friends, these feeble lines
Show, you say, my love declines?   50
To paint ill as I have done,
Proves forgetfulness begun?
Time's gay minions, pleased you see,
Time, your master, governs me;
  Pleased, you mock the fruitless cry:
  'Quick, thy tablets, Memory!'

Ah, too true! Time's current strong
Leaves us fixed to nothing long.
Yet, if little stays with man,
Ah, retain we all we can!   60
If the clear impression dies,
Ah, the dim remembrance prize!
  Ere the parting hour go by,
  Quick, thy tablets, Memory!

Switzerland

1 MEETING

Again I see my bliss at hand,
The town, the lake are here;
My Marguerite smiles upon the strand,
Unaltered with the year.

I know that graceful figure fair,
That cheek of languid hue;
I know that soft, enkerchiefed hair,
And those sweet eyes of blue.

Again I spring to make my choice;
Again in tones of ire
I hear a God's tremendous voice:
'Be counselled, and retire.'

Ye guiding Powers who join and part,
What would ye have with me?
Ah, warn some more ambitious heart,
And let the peaceful be!

2 PARTING

Ye storm-winds of Autumn!
Who rush by, who shake
The window, and ruffle
The gleam-lighted lake;
Who cross to the hill-side
Thin-sprinkled with farms,
Where the high woods strip sadly
Their yellowing arms –
Ye are bound for the mountains!

Ah! with you let me go   10
Where your cold, distant barrier,
The vast range of snow,
Through the loose clouds lifts dimly
Its white peaks in air –
How deep is their stillness!
Ah, would I were there!

But on the stairs what voice is this I hear,
Buoyant as morning, and as morning clear?
Say, has some wet bird-haunted English lawn
Lent it the music of its trees at dawn?   20
Or was it from some sun-flecked mountain-brook
That the sweet voice its upland clearness took?
        Ah! it comes nearer –
        Sweet notes, this way!

    Hark! fast by the window
    The rushing winds go,
    To the ice-cumbered gorges,
    The vast seas of snow!

    There the torrents drive upward
    Their rock-strangled hum;   30
    There the avalanche thunders
    The hoarse torrent dumb.
    – I come, O ye mountains!
    Ye torrents, I come!

But who is this, by the half-opened door,
Whose figure casts a shadow on the floor?
The sweet blue eyes – the soft, ash-coloured hair –
The cheeks that still their gentle paleness wear –
The lovely lips, with their arch smile that tells
The unconquered joy in which her spirit dwells –   40
        Ah! they bend nearer –
        Sweet lips, this way!

Hark! the wind rushes past us!
Ah! with that let me go
To the clear, waning hill-side,
Unspotted by snow,
There to watch, o'er the sunk vale,
The frore mountain-wall,
Where the niched snow-bed sprays down
Its powdery fall.   50
There its dusky blue clusters
The aconite spreads;
There the pines slope, the cloud-strips
Hung soft in their heads.
No life but, at moments,
The mountain-bee's hum.
– I come, O ye mountains!
Ye pine-woods, I come!

Forgive me! forgive me!
    Ah, Marguerite, fain   60
Would these arms reach to clasp thee!
    But see! 'tis in vain.

In the void air, towards thee,
    My stretched arms are cast;
But a sea rolls between us –
    Our different past!

To the lips, ah! of others
    Those lips have been pressed,
And others, ere I was,
    Were strained to that breast;   70

Far, far from each other
    Our spirits have grown;
And what heart knows another?
    Ah! who knows his own?

Blow, ye winds! lift me with you!
    I come to the wild.
Fold closely, O Nature!
    Thine arms round thy child.

To thee only God granted
    A heart ever new –
To all always open,
    To all always true.

Ah! calm me, restore me;
    And dry up my tears
On thy high mountain-platforms,
    Where morn first appears;

Where the white mists, for ever,
    Are spread and upfurled –
In the stir of the forces
    Whence issued the world.

80

90

3   A FAREWELL

My horse's feet beside the lake,
Where sweet the unbroken moonbeams lay,
Sent echoes through the night to wake
Each glistening strand, each heath-fringed bay.

The poplar avenue was passed,
And the roofed bridge that spans the stream;
Up the steep street I hurried fast,
Led by thy taper's starlike beam.

I came! I saw thee rise! – the blood
Poured flushing to thy languid cheek.

10

Locked in each other's arms we stood,
In tears, with hearts too full to speak.

Days flew; ah, soon I could discern
A trouble in thine altered air!
Thy hand lay languidly in mine,
Thy cheek was grave, thy speech grew rare.

I blame thee not! – this heart, I know,
To be long loved was never framed;
For something in its depths doth glow
Too strange, too restless, too untamed.   20

And women – things that live and move
Mined by the fever of the soul –
They seek to find in those they love
Stern strength, and promise of control.

They ask not kindness, gentle ways –
These they themselves have tried and known;
They ask a soul which never sways
With the blind gusts that shake their own.

I too have felt the load I bore
In a too strong emotion's sway;   30
I too have wished, no woman more,
This starting, feverish heart away.

I too have longed for trenchant force,
And will like a dividing spear;
Have praised the keen, unscrupulous course,
Which knows no doubt, which feels no fear.

But in the world I learnt, what there
Thou too wilt surely one day prove,
That will, that energy, though rare,
Are yet far, far less rare than love.   40

Go, then! – till time and fate impress
This truth on thee, be mine no more!
They will! – for thou, I feel, not less
Than I, wast destined to this lore.

We school our manners, act our parts –
But He, who sees us through and through,
Knows that the bent of both our hearts
Was to be gentle, tranquil, true.

And though we wear out life, alas!
Distracted as a homeless wind,   50
In beating where we must not pass,
In seeking what we shall not find;

Yet we shall one day gain, life past,
Clear prospect o'er our being's whole;
Shall see ourselves, and learn at last
Our true affinities of soul.

We shall not then deny a course
To every thought the mass ignore;
We shall not then call hardness force,
Nor lightness wisdom any more.   60

Then, in the eternal Father's smile,
Our soothed, encouraged souls will dare
To seem as free from pride and guile,
As good, as generous, as they are.

Then we shall know our friends! – though much
Will have been lost – the help in strife,
The thousand sweet, still joys of such
As hand in hand face earthly life –

Though these be lost, there will be yet
A sympathy august and pure;   70

Ennobled by a vast regret,
And by contrition sealed thrice sure.

And we, whose ways were unlike here,
May then more neighbouring courses ply;
May to each other be brought near,
And greet across infinity.

How sweet, unreached by earthly jars,
My sister! to maintain with thee
The hush among the shining stars,
The calm upon the moonlit sea!   80

How sweet to feel, on the boon air,
All our unquiet pulses cease!
To feel that nothing can impair
The gentleness, the thirst for peace –

The gentleness too rudely hurled
On this wild earth of hate and fear;
The thirst for peace a raving world
Would never let us satiate here.

4   ISOLATION. TO MARGUERITE

We were apart; yet, day by day,
I bade my heart more constant be.
I bade it keep the world away,
And grow a home for only thee;
Nor feared but thy love likewise grew,
Like mine, each day, more tried, more true.

The fault was grave! I might have known,
What far too soon, alas! I learned –
The heart can bind itself alone,

And faith may oft be unreturned.   10
Self-swayed our feelings ebb and swell –
Thou lov'st no more; – Farewell! Farewell!

Farewell! – and thou, thou lonely heart,
Which never yet without remorse
Even for a moment didst depart
From thy remote and spheréd course
To haunt the place where passions reign –
Back to thy solitude again!

Back! with the conscious thrill of shame
Which Luna felt, that summer-night,   20
Flash through her pure immortal frame,
When she forsook the starry height
To hang over Endymion's sleep
Upon the pine-grown Latmian steep.

Yet she, chaste queen, had never proved
How vain a thing is mortal love,
Wandering in Heaven, far removed.
But thou hast long had place to prove
This truth – to prove, and make thine own:
'Thou hast been, shalt be, art, alone.'   30

Or, if not quite alone, yet they
Which touch thee are unmating things –
Ocean and clouds and night and day;
Lorn autumns and triumphant springs;
And life, and others' joy and pain,
And love, if love, of happier men.

Of happier men – for they, at least,
Have *dreamed* two human hearts might blend
In one, and were through faith released
From isolation without end   40
Prolonged; nor knew, although not less
Alone than thou, their loneliness.

Yes! in the sea of life enisled,
With echoing straits between us thrown,
Dotting the shoreless watery wild,
We mortal millions live *alone*.
The islands feel the enclasping flow,
And then their endless bounds they know.

But when the moon their hollows lights,
And they are swept by balms of spring,
And in their glens, on starry nights,
The nightingales divinely sing;   10
And lovely notes, from shore to shore,
Across the sounds and channels pour –

Oh! then a longing like despair
Is to their farthest caverns sent;
For surely once, they feel, we were
Parts of a single continent!
Now round us spreads the watery plain –
Oh might our marges meet again!

Who ordered, that their longing's fire
Should be, as soon as kindled, cooled?   20
Who renders vain their deep desire? –
A God, a God their severance ruled!
And bade betwixt their shores to be
The unplumbed, salt, estranging sea.

6   ABSENCE

In this fair stranger's eyes of grey
Thine eyes, my love! I see.
I shiver; for the passing day
Had borne me far from thee.

This is the curse of life! that not
A nobler, calmer train
Of wiser thoughts and feelings blot
Our passions from our brain;

But each day brings its petty dust
Our soon-choked souls to fill,   10
And we forget because we must
And not because we will.

I struggle towards the light; and ye,
Once-longed-for storms of love!
If with the light ye cannot be,
I bear that ye remove.

I struggle towards the light – but oh,
While yet the night is chill,
Upon time's barren, stormy flow,
Stay with me, Marguerite, still!   20

Ten years! and to my waking eye
Once more the roofs of Berne appear;
The rocky banks, the terrace high,
The stream! – and do I linger here?

The clouds are on the Oberland,
The Jungfrau snows look faint and far;
But bright are those green fields at hand,
And through those fields comes down the Aar,

And from the blue twin-lakes it comes,
Flows by the town, the churchyard fair;   10
And 'neath the garden-walk it hums,
The house! – and is my Marguerite there?

Ah, shall I see thee, while a flush
Of startled pleasure floods thy brow,
Quick through the oleanders brush,
And clap thy hands, and cry: '*Tis thou!*

Or hast thou long since wandered back,
Daughter of France! to France, thy home;
And flitted down the flowery track
Where feet like thine too lightly come?   20

Doth riotous laughter now replace
Thy smile; and rouge, with stony glare,
Thy cheek's soft hue; and fluttering lace
The kerchief that enwound thy hair?

Or is it over? – art thou dead?
Dead! – and no warning shiver ran
Across my heart, to say thy thread
Of life was cut, and closed thy span!

Could from earth's ways that figure slight
Be lost, and I not feel 'twas so?   30
Of that fresh voice the gay delight
Fail from earth's air, and I not know?

Or shall I find thee still, but changed,
But not the Marguerite of thy prime?
With all thy being re-arranged,
Passed through the crucible of time;

With spirit vanished, beauty waned,
And hardly yet a glance, a tone,
A gesture – anything – retained
Of all that was my Marguerite's own?   40

I will not know! For wherefore try,
To things by mortal course that live,
A shadow durability,
For which they were not meant, to give?

Like driftwood spars, which meet and pass
Upon the boundless ocean-plain,
So on the sea of life, alas!
Man meets man – meets, and quits again.

I knew it when my life was young;
I feel it still, now youth is o'er.   50
– The mists are on the mountain hung,
And Marguerite I shall see no more.

Stanzas in Memory of the Author of 'Obermann'

In front the awful Alpine track
Crawls up its rocky stair;
The autumn storm-winds drive the rack,
Close o'er it, in the air.

Behind are the abandoned baths
Mute in their meadows lone;
The leaves are on the valley paths,
The mists are on the Rhone –

The white mists rolling like a sea!
I hear the torrents roar.   10
– Yes, Obermann, all speaks of thee;
I feel thee near once more!

I turn thy leaves! I feel their breath
Once more upon me roll;
That air of languor, cold, and death,
    Which brooded o'er thy soul.

Fly hence, poor wretch, whoe'er thou art,
Condemned to cast about,
All shipwreck in thy own weak heart,
For comfort from without!   20

A fever in these pages burns
Beneath the calm they feign;
A wounded human spirit turns,
Here, on its bed of pain.

Yes, though the virgin mountain-air
Fresh through these pages blows;
Though to these leaves the glaciers spare
The soul of their white snows;

Though here a mountain-murmur swells
Of many a dark-boughed pine;   30
Though, as you read, you hear the bells
Of the high-pasturing kine –

Yet, through the hum of torrent lone,
And brooding mountain-bee,
There sobs I know not what ground-tone
Of human agony.

Is it for this, because the sound
Is fraught too deep with pain,
That Obermann! the world around
So little loves thy strain?   40

Some secrets may the poet tell,
For the world loves new ways;
To tell too deep ones is not well –
It knows not what he says.

Yet, of the spirits who have reigned
In this our troubled day,
I know but two, who have attained,
Save thee, to see their way.

By England's lakes, in grey old age,
His quiet home one keeps;   50
And one, the strong much-toiling sage,
In German Weimar sleeps.

But Wordsworth's eyes avert their ken
From half of human fate;
And Goethe's course few sons of men
May think to emulate.

For he pursued a lonely road,
His eyes on Nature's plan;

Neither made man too much a God,
Nor God too much a man. 60

Strong was he, with a spirit free
From mists, and sane, and clear;
Clearer, how much! than ours – yet we
Have a worse course to steer.

For though his manhood bore the blast
Of a tremendous time,
Yet in a tranquil world was passed
His tenderer youthful prime.

But we, brought forth and reared in hours
Of change, alarm, surprise – 70
What shelter to grow ripe is ours?
What leisure to grow wise?

Like children bathing on the shore,
Buried a wave beneath,
Their second wave succeeds, before
We have had time to breathe.

Too fast we live, too much are tried,
Too harassed, to attain
Wordsworth's sweet calm, or Goethe's wide
And luminous view to gain. 80

And then we turn, thou sadder sage,
To thee! we feel thy spell!
– The hopeless tangle of our age,
Thou too hast scanned it well!

Immoveable thou sittest, still
As death, composed to bear!
Thy head is clear, thy feeling chill,
And icy thy despair.

Yes, as the son of Thetis said,
I hear thee saying now: 90
Greater by far than thou are dead;
Strive not! die also thou!

Ah! two desires toss about
The poet's feverish blood.
One drives him to the world without,
And one to solitude.

The glow, he cries, *the thrill of life,*
Where, where do these abound?
Not in the world, not in the strife
Of men, shall they be found. 100

He who hath watched, not shared, the strife,
Knows how the day hath gone.
He only lives with the world's life,
Who hath renounced his own.

To thee we come, then! Clouds are rolled
Where thou, O seer! art set;
Thy realm of thought is drear and cold –
The world is colder yet!

And thou hast pleasures, too, to share
With those who come to thee – 110
Balms floating on thy mountain-air,
And healing sights to see.

How often, where the slopes are green
On Jaman, hast thou sate
By some high chalet-door, and seen
The summer-day grow late;

And darkness steal o'er the wet grass
With the pale crocus starred,

And reach that glimmering sheet of glass
Beneath the piny sward,   120

Lake Leman's waters, far below!
And watched the rosy light
Fade from the distant peaks of snow;
And on the air of night

Heard accents of the eternal tongue
Through the pine branches play –
Listened, and felt thyself grown young!
Listened and wept – Away!

Away the dreams that but deceive
And thou, sad guide, adieu!   130
I go, fate drives me; but I leave
Half of my life with you.

We, in some unknown Power's employ,
Move on a rigorous line;
Can neither, when we will, enjoy,
Nor, when we will, resign.

I in the world must live; but thou,
Thou melancholy shade!
Wilt not, if thou canst see me now,
Condemn me, nor upbraid.   140

For thou art gone away from earth,
And place with those dost claim,
The Children of the Second Birth,
Whom the world could not tame;

And with that small, transfigured band,
Whom many a different way
Conducted to their common land,
Thou learn'st to think as they.

Christian and pagan, king and slave,
Soldier and anchorite,   150
Distinctions we esteem so grave,
Are nothing in their sight.

They do not ask, who pined unseen,
Who was on action hurled,
Whose one bond is, that all have been
Unspotted by the world.

There without anger thou wilt see
Him who obeys thy spell
No more, so he but rest, like thee,
Unsoiled! – and so, farewell.   160

Farewell! – Whether thou now liest near
That much-loved inland sea,
The ripples of whose blue waves cheer
Vevey and Meillerie;

And in that gracious region bland,
Where with clear-rustling wave
The scented pines of Switzerland
Stand dark round thy green grave,

Between the dusty vineyard-walls
Issuing on that green place   170
The early peasant still recalls
The pensive stranger's face,

And stoops to clear thy moss-grown date
Ere he plods on again;
Or whether, by maligner fate,
Among the swarms of men,

Where between granite terraces
The blue Seine rolls her wave,

The Capital of Pleasure sees
The hardly-heard-of grave;

Farewell! Under the sky we part,
In this stern Alpine dell.
O unstrung will! O broken heart!
A last, a last farewell!

Empedocles on Etna

A DRAMATIC POEM

Persons

EMPEDOCLES
PAUSANIAS, *a Physician.*
CALLICLES, *a young Harp-player.*

*The Scene of the Poem is on Mount Etna; at first in the forest region,
afterwards on the summit of the mountain.*

ACT I. SCENE I

Morning. A Pass in the forest region of Etna.

CALLICLES

(Alone, resting on a rock by the path.)

The mules, I think, will not be here this hour;
They feel the cool wet turf under their feet
By the stream-side, after the dusty lanes
In which they have toiled all night from Catana,
And scarcely will they budge a yard. O Pan,
How gracious is the mountain at this hour!
A thousand times have I been here alone,
Or with the revellers from the mountain-towns,

But never on so fair a morn; the sun
Is shining on the brilliant mountain-crests,   10
And on the highest pines; but farther down,
Here in the valley, is in shade; the sward
Is dark, and on the stream the mist still hangs;
One sees one's footprints crushed in the wet grass,
One's breath curls in the air; and on these pines
That climb from the stream's edge, the long grey tufts,
Which the goats love, are jewelled thick with dew.
Here will I stay till the slow litter comes.
I have my harp too – that is well. Apollo!
What mortal could be sick or sorry here?   20
I know not in what mind Empedocles,
Whose mules I followed, may be coming up,
But if, as most men say, he is half mad
With exile, and with brooding on his wrongs,
Pausanias, his sage friend, who mounts with him,
Could scarce have lighted on a lovelier cure.
The mules must be below, far down. I hear
Their tinkling bells, mixed with the song of birds,
Rise faintly to me – now it stops! Who's here?
Pausanias! and on foot? alone?

Pausanias

              And thou, then?   30
I left thee supping with Peisianax,
With thy head full of wine, and thy hair crowned,
Touching thy harp as the whim came on thee,
And praised and spoiled by master and by guests
Almost as much as the new dancing-girl.
Why hast thou followed us?

Callicles

             The night was hot,
And the feast past its prime; so we slipped out,
Some of us, to the portico to breathe –
Peisianax, thou know'st, drinks late; and then,

67

As I was lifting my soiled garland off,   40
I saw the mules and litter in the court,
And in the litter sate Empedocles;
Thou, too, wast with him. Straightway I sped home;
I saddled my white mule, and all night long
Through the cool lovely country followed you,
Passed you a little since as morning dawned,
And have this hour sate by the torrent here,
Till the slow mules should climb in sight again.
And now?

Pausanias
        And now, back to the town with speed!
Crouch in the wood first, till the mules have passed;   50
They do but halt, they will be here anon.
Thou must be viewless to Empedocles;
Save mine, he must not meet a human eye.
One of his moods is on him that thou know'st;
I think, thou wouldst not vex him.

Callicles
                 No – and yet
I would fain stay, and help thee tend him. Once
He knew me well, and would oft notice me;
And still, I know not how, he draws me to him,
And I could watch him with his proud sad face,
His flowing locks and gold-encircled brow   60
And kingly gait, for ever; such a spell
In his severe looks, such a majesty
As drew of old the people after him,
In Agrigentum and Olympia,
When his star reigned, before his banishment,
Is potent still on me in his decline.
But oh! Pausanias, he is changed of late;
There is a settled trouble in his air
Admits no momentary brightening now,
And when he comes among his friends at feasts,   70

'Tis as an orphan among prosperous boys.
Thou know'st of old he loved this harp of mine,
When first he sojourned with Peisianax;
He is now always moody, and I fear him;
But I would serve him, soothe him, if I could,
Dared one but try.

Pausanias
　　　　Thou wast a kind child ever!
He loves thee, but he must not see thee now.
Thou hast indeed a rare touch on thy harp,
He loves that in thee, too; there was a time
(But that is passed), he would have paid thy strain   80
With music to have drawn the stars from heaven.
He hath his harp and laurel with him still,
But he has laid the use of music by,
And all which might relax his settled gloom.
Yet thou may'st try thy playing, if thou wilt –
But thou must keep unseen; follow us on,
But at a distance! in these solitudes,
In this clear mountain-air, a voice will rise,
Though from afar, distinctly; it may soothe him.
Play when we halt, and, when the evening comes   90
And I must leave him (for his pleasure is
To be left musing these soft nights alone
In the high unfrequented mountain-spots),
Then watch him, for he ranges swift and far,
Sometimes to Etna's top, and to the cone;
But hide thee in the rocks a great way down,
And try thy noblest strains, my Callicles,
With the sweet night to help thy harmony!
Thou wilt earn my thanks sure, and perhaps his.

Callicles
More than a day and night, Pausanias,   100
Of this fair summer-weather, on these hills,
Would I bestow to help Empedocles.

69

That needs no thanks; one is far better here
Than in the broiling city in these heats.
But tell me, how hast thou persuaded him
In this his present fierce, man-hating mood,
To bring thee out with him alone on Etna?

Pausanias
Thou hast heard all men speaking of Pantheia,
The woman who at Agrigentum lay
Thirty long days in a cold trance of death,   110
And whom Empedocles called back to life.
Thou art too young to note it, but his power
Swells with the swelling evil of this time,
And holds men mute to see where it will rise.
He could stay swift diseases in old days,
Chain madmen by the music of his lyre,
Cleanse to sweet airs the breath of poisonous streams,
And in the mountain-chinks inter the winds.
This he could do of old; but now, since all
Clouds and grows daily worse in Sicily,   120
Since broils tear us in twain, since this new swarm
Of sophists has got empire in our schools
Where he was paramount, since he is banished
And lives a lonely man in triple gloom –
He grasps the very reins of life and death.
I asked him of Pantheia yesterday,
When we were gathered with Peisianax,
And he made answer, I should come at night
On Etna here, and be alone with him,
And he would tell me, as his old, tried friend,   130
Who still was faithful, what might profit me;
That is, the secret of this miracle.

Callicles
Bah! Thou a doctor! Thou art superstitious.
Simple Pausanias, 'twas no miracle!
Pantheia, for I know her kinsmen well,

Was subject to these trances from a girl.
Empedocles would say so, did he deign;
But he still lets the people, whom he scorns,
Gape and cry *wizard* at him, if they list.
But thou, thou art no company for him!   140
Thou art as cross, as soured as himself!
Thou hast some wrong from thine own citizens,
And then thy friend is banished, and on that,
Straightway thou fallest to arraign the times,
As if the sky was impious not to fall.
The sophists are no enemies of his;
I hear, Gorgias, their chief, speaks nobly of him,
As of his gifted master, and once friend.
He is too scornful, too high-wrought, too bitter.
'Tis not the times, 'tis not the sophists vex him;   150
There is some root of suffering in himself,
Some secret and unfollowed vein of woe,
Which makes the time look black and sad to him.
Pester him not in this his sombre mood
With questionings about an idle tale,
But lead him through the lovely mountain-paths,
And keep his mind from preying on itself,
And talk to him of things at hand and common,
Not miracles! thou art a learned man,
But credulous of fables as a girl.   160

Pausanias

And thou, a boy whose tongue outruns his knowledge,
And on whose lightness blame is thrown away.
Enough of this! I see the litter wind
Up by the torrent-side, under the pines.
I must rejoin Empedocles. Do thou
Crouch in the brushwood till the mules have passed;
Then play thy kind part well. Farewell till night!

71

SCENE II

Noon. A Glen on the highest skirts of the woody region of Etna.
EMPEDOCLES – PAUSANIAS

Pausanias
The noon is hot. When we have crossed the stream,
We shall have left the woody tract, and come
Upon the open shoulder of the hill.
See how the giant spires of yellow bloom
Of the sun-loving gentian, in the heat,
Are shining on those naked slopes like flame!
Let us rest here; and now, Empedocles,
Pantheia's history!

[*A harp-note below is heard*

Empedocles
                    Hark! what sound was that
Rose from below? If it were possible,
And we were not so far from human haunt,   10
I should have said that some one touched a harp.
Hark! there again!

Pausanias
                    'Tis the boy Callicles,
The sweetest harp-player in Catana.
He is for ever coming on these hills,
In summer, to all country-festivals,
With a gay revelling band; he breaks from them
Sometimes, and wanders far among the glens.
But heed him not, he will not mount to us;
I spoke with him this morning. Once more, therefore,
Instruct me of Pantheia's story, Master,
As I have prayed thee.

Empedocles
                    That? and to what end?

72

Pausanias

It is enough that all men speak of it.
But I will also say, that when the Gods
Visit us as they do with sign and plague,
To know those spells of thine which stay their hand
Were to live free from terror.

Empedocles
                    Spells? Mistrust them!
Mind is the spell which governs earth and heaven.
Man has a mind with which to plan his safety;
Know that, and help thyself!

Pausanias
                    But thine own words?
'The wit and counsel of man was never clear,   30
Troubles confound the little wit he has.'
Mind is a light which the Gods mock us with,
To lead those false who trust it.
                         [*The harp sounds again.*

Empedocles
                    Hist! once more!
Listen, Pausanias! – Ay, 'tis Callicles;
I know these notes among a thousand. Hark!

Callicles
(*Sings unseen, from below*)
The track winds down to the clear stream,
To cross the sparkling shallows; there
The cattle love to gather, on their way
To the high mountain-pastures, and to stay,
Till the rough cow-herds drive them past,   40
Knee-deep in the cool ford; for 'tis the last
Of all the woody, high, well-watered dells
On Etna; and the beam
Of noon is broken there by chestnut-boughs

Down its steep verdant sides; the air
Is freshened by the leaping stream, which throws
Eternal showers of spray on the mossed roots
Of trees, and veins of turf, and long dark shoots
Of ivy-plants, and fragrant hanging bells
Of hyacinths, and on late anemones,   50
That muffle its wet banks; but glade,
And stream, and sward, and chestnut-trees,
End here; Etna beyond, in the broad glare
Of the hot noon, without a shade,
Slope behind slope, up to the peak, lies bare;
The peak, round which the white clouds play.

In such a glen, on such a day,
On Pelion, on the grassy ground,
Chiron, the aged Centaur lay,
The young Achilles standing by.   60
The Centaur taught him to explore
The mountains; where the glens are dry
And the tired Centaurs come to rest,
And where the soaking springs abound
And the straight ashes grow for spears,
And where the hill-goats come to feed,
And the sea-eagles build their nest.
He showed him Phthia far away,
And said: O boy, I taught this lore
To Peleus, in long distant years!   70
He told him of the Gods, the stars,
The tides; and then of mortal wars,
And of the life which heroes lead
Before they reach the Elysian place
And rest in the immortal mead;
And all the wisdom of his race.

The music below ceases, and EMPEDOCLES *speaks, accompanying
himself in a solemn manner on his harp.*

The out-spread world to span
A cord the Gods first slung,
And then the soul of man
There, like a mirror, hung,   80
And bade the winds through space impel the gusty toy.

Hither and thither spins
The wind-borne, mirroring soul,
A thousand glimpses wins,
And never sees a whole;
Looks once, and drives elsewhere, and leaves its last employ.

The Gods laugh in their sleeve
To watch man doubt and fear,
Who knows not what to believe
Since he sees nothing clear,   90
And dares stamp nothing false where he finds nothing sure.

Is this, Pausanias, so?
And can our souls not strive,
But with the winds must go,
And hurry where they drive?
Is fate indeed so strong, man's strength indeed so poor?

I will not judge. That man,
Howbeit, I judge as lost,
Whose mind allows a plan,
Which would degrade it most;   100
And he treats doubt the best who tries to see least ill.

Be not, then, fear's blind slave!
Thou art my friend; to thee,
All knowledge that I have,
All skill I wield, are free.
Ask not the latest news of the last miracle,

Ask not what days and nights
In trance Pantheia lay,
But ask how thou such sights
May'st see without dismay;   110
Ask what most helps when known, thou son of Anchitus!

What? hate, and awe, and shame
Fill thee to see our time;
Thou feelest thy soul's frame
Shaken and out of chime?
What? life and chance go hard with thee too, as with us;

Thy citizens, 'tis said,
Envy thee and oppress,
Thy goodness no men aid,
All strive to make it less;   120
Tyranny, pride, and lust, fill Sicily's abodes;

Heaven is with earth at strife,
Signs make thy soul afraid,
The dead return to life,
Rivers are dried, winds stayed;
Scarce can one think in calm, so threatening are the Gods;

And we feel, day and night,
The burden of ourselves –
Well, then, the wiser wight
In his own bosom delves,   130
And asks what ails him so, and gets what cure he can.

The sophist sneers: Fool, take
Thy pleasure, right or wrong.
The pious wail: Forsake
A world these sophists throng.
Be neither saint nor sophist-led, but be a man!

These hundred doctors try
To preach thee to their school.
We have the truth! they cry;
And yet their oracle,   140
Trumpet it as they will, is but the same as thine.

Once read thy own breast right,
And thou hast done with fears;
Man gets no other light,
Search he a thousand years.
Sink in thyself! there ask what ails thee, at that shrine!

What makes thee struggle and rave?
Why are men ill at ease?
'Tis that the lot they have
Fails their own will to please;   150
For man would make no murmuring, were his will obeyed.

And why is it, that still
Man with his lot thus fights?
'Tis that he makes this *will*
The measure of his *rights*,
And believes Nature outraged if his will's gainsaid.

Couldst thou, Pausanias, learn
How deep a fault is this;
Couldst thou but once discern
Thou hast no *right* to bliss,   160
No title from the Gods to welfare and repose;

Then thou wouldst look less mazed
Whene'er of bliss debarred,
Nor think the Gods were crazed
When thy own lot went hard.
But we are all the same – the fools of our own woes!

For, from the first faint morn
Of life, the thirst for bliss
Deep in man's heart is born;
And, sceptic as he is,   170
He fails not to judge clear if this be quenched or no.

Nor is the thirst to blame.
Man errs not that he deems
His welfare his true aim,
He errs because he dreams
The world does but exist that welfare to bestow.

We mortals are no kings
For each of whom to sway
A new-made world up-springs,
Meant merely for his play;   180
No, we are strangers here; the world is from of old.

In vain our pent wills fret,
And would the world subdue.
Limits we did not set
Condition all we do;
Born into life we are, and life must be our mould.

Born into life! man grows
Forth from his parents' stem,
And blends their bloods, as those
Of theirs are blent in them;   190
So each new man strikes root into a far fore-time.

Born into life! we bring
A bias with us here,
And, when here, each new thing
Affects us we come near;
To tunes we did not call our being must keep chime.

Born into life! in vain,
Opinions, those or these,
Unaltered to retain
The obstinate mind decrees;   200
Experience, like a sea, soaks all-effacing in.

Born into life! who lists
May what is false hold dear,
And for himself make mists
Through which to see less clear;
The world is what it is, for all our dust and din.

Born into life! 'tis we,
And not the world, are new;
Our cry for bliss, our plea,
Others have urged it too –   210
Our wants have all been felt, our errors made before.

No eye could be too sound
To observe a world so vast,
No patience too profound
To sort what's here amassed;
How man may here best live no care too great to explore.

But we – as some rude guest
Would change, where'er he roam,
The manners there professed
To those he brings from home –   220
We mark not the world's course, but would have *it* take *ours*.

The world's course proves the terms
On which man wins content;
Reason the proof confirms –
We spurn it, and invent
A false course for the world, and for ourselves, false powers.

Riches we wish to get,
Yet remain spendthrifts still;
We would have health, and yet
Still use our bodies ill;   230
Bafflers of our own prayers, from youth to life's last scenes.

We would have inward peace,
Yet will not look within;
We would have misery cease,
Yet will not cease from sin;
We want all pleasant ends, but will use no harsh means;

We do not what we ought,
What we ought not, we do,
And lean upon the thought
That chance will bring us through;   240
But our own acts, for good or ill, are mightier powers.

Yet, even when man forsakes
All sin – is just, is pure,
Abandons all which makes
His welfare insecure –
Other existences there are, that clash with ours.

Like us, the lightning-fires
Love to have scope and play;
The stream, like us, desires
An unimpeded way;   250
Like us, the Libyan wind delights to roam at large.

Streams will not curb their pride
The just man not to entomb,
Nor lightnings go aside
To give his virtues room;
Nor is that wind less rough which blows a good man's barge.

Nature, with equal mind,
Sees all her sons at play;
Sees man control the wind,
The wind sweep man away; 260
Allows the proudly-riding and the foundering bark.

And, lastly, though of ours
No weakness spoil our lot,
Though the non-human powers
Of Nature harm us not,
The ill deeds of other men make often *our* life dark.

What were the wise man's plan?
Through this sharp, toil-set life,
To work as best he can,
And win what's won by strife. 270
But we an easier way to cheat our pains have found.

Scratched by a fall, with moans
As children of weak age
Lend life to the dumb stones
Whereon to vent their rage,
And bend their little fists, and rate the senseless ground;

So, loth to suffer mute,
We, peopling the void air,
Make Gods to whom to impute
The ills we ought to bear; 280
With God and Fate to rail at, suffering easily.

Yet grant – as sense long missed
Things that are now perceived,
And much may still exist
Which is not yet believed –
Grant that the world were full of Gods we cannot see;

All things the world which fill
Of but one stuff are spun,
That we who rail are still,
With what we rail at, one;   290
One with the o'erlaboured Power that through the breadth
     and length

Of earth, and air, and sea,
In men, and plants, and stones,
Hath toil perpetually,
And travails, pants and moans;
Fain would do all things well, but sometimes fails in strength.

And patiently exact
This universal God
Alike to any act
Proceeds at any nod,   300
And quietly declaims the cursings of himself.

This is not what man hates,
Yet he can curse but this.
Harsh Gods and hostile Fates
Are dreams! this only *is* –
Is everywhere; sustains the wise, the foolish elf.

Nor only, in the intent
To attach blame elsewhere,
Do we at will invent
Stern Powers who make their care   310
To embitter human life, malignant Deities;

But, next, we would reverse
The scheme ourselves have spun,
And what we made to curse
We now would lean upon,
And feign kind Gods who perfect what man vainly tries.

Look, the world tempts our eye,
And we would know it all!
We map the starry sky,
We mine this earthen ball,   320
We measure the sea-tides, we number the sea-sands;

We scrutinise the dates
Of long-past human things,
The bounds of effaced states,
The lines of deceased kings;
We search out dead men's words, and works of dead men's hands;

We shut our eyes, and muse
How our own minds are made.
What springs of thought they use,
How rightened, how betrayed –   330
And spend our wit to name what most employ unnamed.

But still, as we proceed
The mass swells more and more
Of volumes yet to read,
Of secrets yet to explore.
Our hair grows grey, our eyes are dimmed, our heat is tamed;

We rest our faculties,
And thus address the Gods:
'True science if there is,
It stays in your abodes!   340
Man's measures cannot mete the immeasurable All.

'You only can take in
The world's immense design.
Our desperate search was sin,
Which henceforth we resign,
Sure only that your mind sees all things which befall.'

Fools! That in man's brief term
He cannot all things view,
Affords no ground to affirm
That there are Gods who do;   350
Nor does being weary prove that he has where to rest.

Again. Our youthful blood
Claims rapture as its right;
The world, a rolling flood
Of newness and delight,
Draws in the enamoured gazer to its shining breast;

Pleasure, to our hot grasp,
Gives flowers after flowers;
With passionate warmth we clasp
Hand after hand in ours;   360
Nor do we soon perceive how fast our youth is spent.

At once our eyes grow clear!
We see, in blank dismay,
Year posting after year,
Sense after sense decay;
Our shivering heart is mined by secret discontent;

Yet still, in spite of truth,
In spite of hopes entombed,
That longing of our youth
Burns ever unconsumed,   370
Still hungrier for delights as delights grow more rare.

We pause; we hush our heart,
And thus address the Gods:
'The world hath failed to impart
The joy our youth forebodes,
Failed to fill up the void which in our breasts we bear.

'Changeful till now, we still
Looked on to something new;
Let us, with changeless will,
Henceforth look on to you,   380
To find with you the joy we in vain here require!'

Fools! That so often here
Happiness mocked our prayer.
I think, might make us fear
A like event elsewhere;
Make us, not fly to dreams, but moderate desire.

And yet, for those who know
Themselves, who wisely take
Their way through life, and bow
To what they cannot break,   390
Why should I say that life need yield but *moderate* bliss?

Shall we, with temper spoiled,
Health sapped by living ill,
And judgment all embroiled
By sadness and self-will,
Shall *we* judge what for man is not true bliss or is?

Is it so small a thing
To have enjoyed the sun,
To have lived light in the spring,
To have loved, to have thought, to have done;   400
To have advanced true friends, and beat down baffling foes –

That we must feign a bliss
Of doubtful future date,
And, while we dream on this,
Lose all our present state,
And relegate to worlds yet distant our repose?

Not much, I know, you prize
What pleasures may be had,
Who look on life with eyes
Estranged, like mine, and sad;   410
And yet the village-churl feels the truth more than you

Who's loth to leave this life
Which to him little yields –
His hard-tasked sunburnt wife,
His often-laboured fields,
The boors with whom he talked, the country-spots he knew.

But thou, because thou hear'st
Men scoff at Heaven and Fate,
Because the Gods thou fear'st
Fail to make blest thy state,   420
Tremblest, and wilt not dare to trust the joys there are.

I say: Fear not! Life still
Leaves human effort scope.
But, since life teems with ill,
Nurse no extravagant hope;
Because thou must not dream, thou need'st not then despair!

*A long pause. At the end of it the notes of a harp below are again heard,
and* CALLICLES *sings:–*

Far, far from here,
The Adriatic breaks in a warm bay
Among the green Illyrian hills; and there
The sunshine in the happy glens is fair,   430
And by the sea, and in the brakes.
The grass is cool, the sea-side air
Buoyant and fresh, the mountain flowers
More virginal and sweet than ours.
And there, they say, two bright and aged snakes,
Who once were Cadmus and Harmonia,

86

Bask in the glens or on the warm sea-shore,
In breathless quiet, after all their ills;
Nor do they see their country, nor the place
Where the Sphinx lived among the frowning hills,   440
Nor the unhappy palace of their race,
Nor Thebes, nor the Ismenus, any more.

   There those two live, far in the Illyrian brakes!
They had stayed long enough to see,
In Thebes, the billow of calamity
Over their own dear children rolled,
Curse upon curse, pang upon pang,
For years, they sitting helpless in their home,
A grey old man and woman; yet of old
The Gods had to their marriage come,   450

And at the banquet all the Muses sang.
Therefore they did not end their days
In sight of blood; but were rapt, far away,
To where the west-wind plays,
And murmurs of the Adriatic come
To those untrodden mountain-lawns; and there
Placed safely in changed forms, the pair
Wholly forget their first sad life, and home,
And all the Theban woe, and stray
For ever through the glens, placid and dumb.   460

Empedocles
That was my harp-player again! – where is he?
Down by the stream?

                Pausanias
                Yes, Master, in the wood.

                Empedocles
He ever loved the Theban story well!
But the day wears. Go now, Pausanias,
For I must be alone. Leave me one mule;

87

Take down with thee the rest to Catana.
And for young Callicles, thank him from me;
Tell him, I never failed to love his lyre –
But he must follow me no more to-night.

Pausanias

Thou wilt return to-morrow to the city?   470

Empedocles

Either to-morrow or some other day,
In the sure revolutions of the world,
Good friend, I shall revisit Catana.
I have seen many cities in my time,
Till mine eyes ache with the long spectacle,
And I shall doubtless see them all again;
Thou know'st me for a wanderer from of old.
Meanwhile, stay me not now. Farewell, Pausanias!
            He departs on his way up the mountain.

Pausanias (alone)

I dare not urge him further – he must go;
But he is strangely wrought! I will speed back   480
And bring Peisianax to him from the city;
His counsel could once soothe him. But, Apollo!
How his brow lightened as the music rose!
Callicles must wait here, and play to him;
I saw him through the chestnuts far below,
Just since, down at the stream. Ho! Callicles!
                    He descends, calling.

ACT II

Evening. The Summit of Etna.

EMPEDOCLES

                    Alone! –
On this charred, blackened, melancholy waste,
Crowned by the awful peak, Etna's great mouth,
Round which the sullen vapour rolls – alone!
Pausanias is far hence, and that is well,
For I must henceforth speak no more with man.
He hath his lesson too, and that debt's paid;
And the good, learned, friendly, quiet man
May bravelier front his life, and in himself
Find henceforth energy and heart. But I –   10
The weary man, the banished citizen,
Whose banishment is not his greatest ill,
Whose weariness no energy can reach,
And for whose hurt courage is not the cure –
What should I do with life and living more?

   No, thou art come too late, Empedocles!
And the world hath the day, and must break thee,
Not thou the world. With men thou canst not live,
Their thoughts, their ways, their wishes, are not thine;
And being lonely thou art miserable,   20
For something has impaired thy spirit's strength,
And dried its self-sufficing fount of joy.
Thou canst not live with men nor with thyself –
O sage! O sage! Take then the one way left;
And turn thee to the elements, thy friends,
Thy well-tried friends, thy willing ministers,
And say: Ye helpers, hear Empedocles,
Who asks this final service at your hands!
Before the sophist-brood hath overlaid
The last spark of man's consciousness with words –   30
Ere quite the being of man, ere quite the world
Be disarrayed of their divinity –

Before the soul lose all her solemn joys,
And awe be dead, and hope impossible,
And the soul's deep eternal night come on –
Receive me, hide me, quench me, take me home!

He advances to the edge of the crater. Smoke and fire break forth with a loud noise, and CALLICLES *is heard below singing: –*

The lyre's voice is lovely everywhere;
In the court of Gods, in the city of men,
And in the lonely rock-strewn mountain-glen,
In the still mountain air.   40
Only to Typho it sounds hatefully;
To Typho only, the rebel o'erthrown,
Through whose heart Etna drives her roots of stone
To imbed them in the sea.

Wherefore dost thou groan so loud?
Wherefore do thy nostrils flash,
Through the dark night, suddenly,
Typho, such red jets of flame?
Is thy tortured heart still proud?
Is thy fire-scathed arm still rash?   50
Still alert thy stone-crushed frame?
Doth thy fierce soul still deplore
Thine ancient rout by the Cilician hills,
And that cursed treachery on the Mount of Gore?
Do thy bloodshot eyes still weep
The fight which crowned thine ills,
Thy last mischance on this Sicilian deep?
Hast thou sworn, in thy sad lair,
Where erst the strong sea-currents sucked thee down,
Never to cease to writhe, and try to rest,   60
Letting the sea-stream wander through thy hair?
That thy groans, like thunder pressed,
Begin to roll, and almost drown
The sweet notes whose lulling spell

Gods and the race of mortals love so well,
When through thy caves thou hearest music swell?

But an awful pleasure bland
Spreading o'er the Thunderer's face,
When the sound climbs near his seat,
The Olympian council sees;   70
As he lets his lax right hand,
Which the lightnings doth embrace,
Sink upon his mighty knees.
And the eagle, at the beck
Of the appeasing, gracious harmony,
Droops all his sheeny, brown, deep-feathered neck,
Nestling nearer to Jove's feet;
While o'er his sovran eye
The curtains of the blue films slowly meet
And the white Olympus-peaks   80
Rosily brighten, and the soothed Gods smile
At one another from their golden chairs,
And no one round the charméd circle speaks.
Only the loved Hebe bears
The cup about, whose draughts beguile
Pain and care, with a dark store
Of fresh-pulled violets wreathed and nodding o'er;
And her flushed feet glow on the marble floor.

Empedocles

He fables, yet speaks truth!
The brave, impetuous heart yields everywhere   90
To the subtle, contriving head;
Great qualities are trodden down,
And littleness united
Is become invincible.
These rumblings are not Typho's groans, I know!
These angry smoke-bursts
Are not the passionate breath
Of the mountain-crushed, tortured, intractable Titan king –

91

But over all the world
What suffering is there not seen   100
Of plainness oppressed by cunning,
As the well-counselled Zeus oppressed
That self-helping son of earth!
What anguish of greatness,
Railed and hunted from the world,
Because its simplicity rebukes
This envious, miserable age!

I am weary of it.
– Lie there, ye ensigns
Of my unloved preëminence   110
In an age like this!
Among a people of children,
Who thronged me in their cities,
Who worshipped me in their houses,
And asked, not wisdom,
But drugs to charm with,
But spells to mutter –
All the fool's-armoury of magic! Lie there,
My golden circlet,
My purple robe!   120

Callicles (from below)

As the sky-brightening south-wind clears the day,
And makes the massed clouds roll,
The music of the lyre blows away
The clouds which wrap the soul.
Oh! that Fate had let me see
That triumph of the sweet persuasive lyre,
That famous, final victory,
When jealous Pan with Marsyas did conspire;
When, from far Parnassus' side,
Young Apollo, all the pride   130
Of the Phrygian flutes to tame,
To the Phrygian highlands came;

92

Where the long green reed-beds sway
In the rippled waters grey
Of that solitary lake
Where Mæander's springs are born;
Whence the ridged pine-wooded roots
Of Messogis westward break,
Mounting westward, high and higher.
There was held the famous strife; 140
There the Phrygian brought his flutes,
And Apollo brought his lyre;
And, when now the westering sun
Touched the hills, the strife was done,
And the attentive Muses said:
'Marsyas, thou art vanquishéd!'
Then Apollo's minister
Hanged upon a branching fir
Marsyas, that unhappy Faun,
And began to whet his knife. 150
But the Mænads, who were there,
Left their friend, and with robes flowing
In the wind, and loose dark hair
O'er their polished bosoms blowing,
Each her ribboned tambourine
Flinging on the mountain-sod,
With a lovely frightened mien
Came about the youthful God.
But he turned his beauteous face
Haughtily another way, 160
From the grassy sun-warmed place
Where in proud repose he lay,
With one arm over his head,
Watching how the whetting sped.

   But aloof, on the lake-strand,
Did the young Olympus stand,
Weeping at his master's end;
For the Faun had been his friend.

For he taught him how to sing,
And he taught him flute-playing.   170
Many a morning had they gone
To the glimmering mountain-lakes,
And had torn up by the roots
The tall crested water-reeds
With long plumes and soft brown seeds,
And had carved them into flutes,
Sitting on a tabled stone
Where the shoreward ripple breaks.
And he taught him how to please
The red-snooded Phrygian girls,   180
Whom the summer evening sees
Flashing in the dance's whirls
Underneath the starlit trees
In the mountain-villages.
Therefore now Olympus stands,
At his master's piteous cries
Pressing fast with both his hands
His white garment to his eyes,
Not to see Apollo's scorn;
Ah, poor Faun, poor Faun! ah, poor Faun!   190

Empedocles

And lie thou there,
My laurel bough!
Scornful Apollo's ensign, lie thou there!
Though thou hast been my shade in the world's heat –
Though I have loved thee, lived in honouring thee –
Yet lie thou there,
My laurel bough!
I am weary of thee.
I am weary of the solitude
Where he who bears thee must abide –   200
Of the rocks of Parnassus,
Of the gorge of Delphi,
Of the moonlit peaks, and the caves.

Thou guardest them, Apollo!
Over the grave of the slain Pytho,
Though young, intolerably severe!
Thou keepest aloof the profane,
But the solitude oppresses thy votary!
The jars of men reach him not in thy valley –
But can life reach him?   210
Thou fencest him from the multitude –
Who will fence him from himself?
He hears nothing but the cry of the torrents,
And the beating of his own heart.
The air is thin, the veins swell,
The temples tighten and throb there –
Air! air!

Take thy bough, set me free from my solitude;
I have been enough alone!

Where shall thy votary fly then? back to men? 220
But they will gladly welcome him once more,
And help him to unbend his too tense thought,
And rid him of the presence of himself,
And keep their friendly chatter at his ear,
And haunt him, till the absence from himself,
That other torment, grow unbearable;
And he will fly to solitude again,
And he will find its air too keen for him,
And so change back; and many thousand times
Be miserably bandied to and fro   230
Like a sea-wave, betwixt the world and thee,
Thou young, implacable God! and only death
Can cut his oscillations short, and so
Bring him to poise. There is no other way.

And yet what days were those, Parmenides!
When we were young, when we could number friends
In all the Italian cities like ourselves,

When with elated hearts we joined your train,
Ye Sun-born Virgins! on the road of truth.
Then we could still enjoy, then neither thought   240
Nor outward things were closed and dead to us:
But we received the shock of mighty thoughts
On simple minds with a pure natural joy;
And if the sacred load oppressed our brain,
We had the power to feel the pressure eased,
The brow unbound, the thoughts flow free again,
In the delightful commerce of the world.
We had not lost our balance then, nor grown
Thought's slaves, and dead to every natural joy.
The smallest thing could give us pleasure then –   250
The sports of the country-people,
A flute-note from the woods,
Sunset over the sea;
Seed-time and harvest,
The reapers in the corn,
The vinedresser in his vineyard,
The village-girl at her wheel.

Fullness of life and power of feeling, ye
Are for the happy, for the souls at ease,
Who dwell on a firm basis of content!   260
But he, who has outlived his prosperous days –
But he, whose youth fell on a different world
From that on which his exiled age is thrown –
Whose mind was fed on other food, was trained
By other rules than are in vogue to-day –
Whose habit of thought is fixed, who will not change,
But, in a world he loves not, must subsist
In ceaseless opposition, be the guard
Of his own breast, fettered to what he guards,
That the world win no mastery over him –   270
Who has no friend, no fellow left, not one;
Who has no minute's breathing space allowed
To nurse his dwindling faculty of joy –

Joy and the outward world must die to him,
As they are dead to me.

A long pause, during which EMPEDOCLES *remains motionless,
plunged in thought. The night deepens. He moves forward
and gazes round him, and proceeds:–*

And you, ye stars,
Who slowly begin to marshal,
As of old, in the fields of heaven,
Your distant, melancholy lines!
Have you, too, survived yourselves?   280
Are you, too, what I fear to become?
You, too, once lived;
You, too, moved joyfully
Among august companions,
In an older world, peopled by Gods,
In a mightier order,
The radiant, rejoicing, intelligent Sons of Heaven.
But now, ye kindle
Your lonely, cold-shining lights,
Unwilling lingerers   290
In the heavenly wilderness,
For a younger, ignoble world;
And renew, by necessity,
Night after night your courses,
In echoing, unneared silence,
Above a race you know not –
Uncaring and undelighted,
Without friend and without home;
Weary like us, though not
Weary with our weariness.   300

No, no, ye stars! there is no death with you,
No languor, no decay! languor and death,
They are with me, not you! ye are alive –
Ye, and the pure dark ether where ye ride

97

Brilliant above me! And thou, fiery world,
That sapp'st the vitals of this terrible mount
Upon whose charred and quaking crust I stand –
Thou, too, brimmest with life! – the sea of cloud,
That heaves its white and billowy vapours up
To moat this isle of ashes from the world,   310
Lives; and that other fainter sea, far down,
O'er whose lit floor a road of moonbeams leads
To Etna's Liparëan sister-fires
And the long dusky line of Italy –
That mild and luminous floor of waters lives,
With held-in joy swelling its heart; I only,
Whose spring of hope is dried, whose spirit has failed,
I, who have not, like these, in solitude
Maintained courage and force, and in myself
Nursed an immortal vigour – I alone   320
Am dead to life and joy, therefore I read
In all things my own deadness.

A long silence. He continues:–

Oh, that I could glow like this mountain!
Oh, that my heart bounded with the swell of the sea!
Oh, that my soul were full of light as the stars!
Oh, that it brooded over the world like the air!

But no, this heart will glow no more; thou art
A living man no more, Empedocles!
Nothing but a devouring flame of thought –
But a naked, eternally restless mind!   330

After a pause:–

To the elements it came from
Everything will return –
Our bodies to earth,
Our blood to water,

98

Heat to fire,
Breath to air.
They were well born, they will be well entombed –
But mind? . . .

And we might gladly share the fruitful stir
Down in our mother earth's miraculous womb;   340
Well would it be
With what rolled of us in the stormy main;
We might have joy, blent with the all-bathing air,
Or with the nimble, radiant life of fire.

But mind, but thought –
If these have been the master part of us –
Where will *they* find their parent element?
What will receive *them*, who will call *them* home?
But we shall still be in them, and they in us,
And we shall be the strangers of the world,   350
And they will be our lords, as they are now;
And keep us prisoners of our consciousness,
And never let us clasp and feel the All
But through their forms, and modes, and stifling veils.
And we shall be unsatisfied as now;
And we shall feel the agony of thirst,
The ineffable longing for the life of life
Baffled for ever; and still thought and mind
Will hurry us with them on their homeless march,
Over the unallied unopening earth,   360
Over the unrecognising sea; while air
Will blow us fiercely back to sea and earth,
And fire repel us from its living waves.
And then we shall unwillingly return
Back to this meadow of calamity,
This uncongenial place, this human life;
And in our individual human state
Go through the sad probation all again,
To see if we will poise our life at last,

99

To see if we will now at last be true   370
To our own only true, deep-buried selves,
Being one with which we are one with the whole world;
Or whether we will once more fall away
Into some bondage of the flesh or mind,
Some slough of sense, or some fantastic maze
Forged by the imperious lonely thinking-power.
And each succeeding age in which we are born
Will have more peril for us than the last;
Will goad our senses with a sharper spur,
Will fret our minds to an intenser play,   380
Will make ourselves harder to be discerned.
And we shall struggle awhile, gasp and rebel –
And we shall fly for refuge to past times,
Their soul of unworn youth, their breath of greatness;
And the reality will pluck us back,
Knead us in its hot hand, and change our nature.
And we shall feel our powers of effort flag,
And rally them for one last fight – and fail;
And we shall sink in the impossible strife,
And be astray for ever.

                    Slave of sense   390
I have in no wise been; but slave of thought? . . .
And who can say: I have been always free,
Lived ever in the light of my own soul? –
I cannot; I have lived in wrath and gloom,
Fierce, disputatious, ever at war with man,
Far from my own soul, far from warmth and light.
But I have not grown easy in these bonds –
But I have not denied what bonds these were.
Yea, I take myself to witness,
That I have loved no darkness,   400
Sophisticated no truth,
Nursed no delusion,
Allowed no fear!

And therefore, O ye elements! I know –
Ye know it too – it hath been granted me
Not to die wholly, not to be all enslaved.
I feel it in this hour. The numbing cloud
Mounts off my soul: I feel it, I breathe free.

Is it but for a moment?
– Ah, boil up, ye vapours!   410
Leap and roar, thou sea of fire!
My soul glows to meet you.
Ere it flag, ere the mists
Of despondency and gloom
Rush over it again,
Receive me, save me!

He plunges into the crater.

Callicles
(from below)
Through the black, rushing smoke-bursts,
Thick breaks the red flame;
All Etna heaves fiercely
Her forest-clothed frame.   420

Not here, O Apollo!
Are haunts meet for thee.
But, where Helicon breaks down
In cliff to the sea,

Where the moon-silvered inlets
Send far their light voice
Up the still vale of Thisbe,
O speed, and rejoice!

On the sward at the cliff-top
Lie strewn the white flocks,   430
On the cliff-side the pigeons
Roost deep in the rocks.

In the moonlight the shepherds,
Soft lulled by the rills,
Lie wrapped in their blankets
Asleep on the hills.

– What forms are these coming
So white through the gloom?
What garments out-glistening
The gold-flowered broom?   440

What sweet-breathing presence
Out-perfumes the thyme?
What voices enrapture
The night's balmy prime?

'Tis Apollo comes leading
His choir, the Nine.
– The leader is fairest,
But all are divine.

They are lost in the hollows!
They stream up again!   450
What seeks on this mountain
The glorified train?

They bathe on this mountain,
In the spring by their road;
Then on to Olympus,
Their endless abode.

– Whose praise do they mention?
Of what is it told?
What will be for ever;
What was from of old.   460

First hymn they the Father
Of all things; and then,

The rest of immortals,
The action of men.

The day in his hotness,
The strife with the palm;
The night in her silence,
The stars in their calm.

Memorial Verses

Goethe in Weimar sleeps, and Greece,
Long since, saw Byron's struggle cease.
But one such death remained to come;
The last poetic voice is dumb –
We stand to-day by Wordsworth's tomb.

When Byron's eyes were shut in death,
We bowed our head and held our breath.
He taught us little; but our soul
Had *felt* him like the thunder's roll.
With shivering heart the strife we saw   10
Of passion with eternal law;
And yet with reverential awe
We watched the fount of fiery life
Which served for that Titanic strife.

    When Goethe's death was told, we said:
Sunk, then, is Europe's sagest head.
Physician of the iron age,
Goethe has done his pilgrimage.
He took the suffering human race,
He read each wound, each weakness clear;   20
And struck his finger on the place,

And said: *Thou ailest here, and here!*
He looked on Europe's dying hour
Of fitful dream and feverish power;
His eye plunged down the weltering strife,
The turmoil of expiring life –
He said: *The end is everywhere,*
Art still has truth, take refuge there!
And he was happy, if to know
Causes of things, and far below   30
His feet to see the lurid flow
Of terror, and insane distress,
And headlong fate, be happiness.

And Wordsworth! – Ah, pale ghosts, rejoice!
For never has such soothing voice
Been to your shadowy world conveyed,
Since erst, at morn, some wandering shade
Heard the clear song of Orpheus come
Through Hades, and the mournful gloom.
Wordsworth has gone from us – and ye,   40
Ah, may ye feel his voice as we!
He too upon a wintry clime
Had fallen – on this iron time
Of doubts, disputes, distractions, fears.
He found us when the age had bound
Our souls in its benumbing round;
He spoke, and loosed our heart in tears.
He laid us as we lay at birth
On the cool flowery lap of earth,
Smiles broke from us and we had ease;   50
The hills were round us, and the breeze
Went o'er the sun-lit fields again;
Our foreheads felt the wind and rain.
Our youth returned; for there was shed
On spirits that had long been dead,
Spirits dried up and closely furled,
The freshness of the early world.

Ah! since dark days still bring to light
Man's prudence and man's fiery might,
Time may restore us in his course   60
Goethe's sage mind and Byron's force;
But where will Europe's latter hour
Again find Wordsworth's healing power?
Others will teach us how to dare,
And against fear our breast to steel;
Others will strengthen us to bear –
But who, ah! who, will make us feel?
The cloud of mortal destiny,
Others will front it fearlessly –
But who, like him, will put it by?   70

Keep fresh the grass upon his grave,
O Rotha, with thy living wave!
Sing him thy best! for few or none
Hears thy voice right, now he is gone.

Dover Beach

The sea is calm to-night.
The tide is full, the moon lies fair
Upon the straits; on the French coast the light
Gleams and is gone; the cliffs of England stand,
Glimmering and vast, out in the tranquil bay.
Come to the window, sweet is the night-air!
Only, from the long line of spray
Where the sea meets the moon-blanched land,
Listen! you hear the grating roar
Of pebbles which the waves draw back, and fling,   10
At their return, up the high strand,
Begin, and cease, and then again begin,

With tremulous cadence slow, and bring
The eternal note of sadness in.

Sophocles long ago
Heard it on the Ægæan, and it brought
Into his mind the turbid ebb and flow
Of human misery; we
Find also in the sound a thought,
Hearing it by this distant northern sea.   20

The Sea of Faith
Was once, too, at the full, and round earth's shore
Lay like the folds of a bright girdle furled.
But now I only hear
Its melancholy, long, withdrawing roar,
Retreating, to the breath
Of the night-wind, down the vast edges drear
And naked shingles of the world.

Ah, love, let us be true
To one another! for the world, which seems   30
To lie before us like a land of dreams,
So various, so beautiful, so new,
Hath really neither joy, nor love, nor light,
Nor certitude, nor peace, nor help for pain:
And we are here as on a darkling plain
Swept with confused alarms of struggle and flight,
Where ignorant armies clash by night.

The Youth of Nature

Raised are the dripping oars,
Silent the boat! the lake,
Lovely and soft as a dream,
Swims in the sheen of the moon.
The mountains stand at its head
Clear in the pure June-night,
But the valleys are flooded with haze.
Rydal and Fairfield are there;
In the shadow Wordsworth lies dead.
So it is, so it will be for aye.   10
Nature is fresh as of old,
Is lovely; a mortal is dead.

The spots which recall him survive,
For he lent a new life to these hills.
The Pillar still broods o'er the fields
Which border Ennerdale Lake,
And Egremont sleeps by the sea.
The gleam of The Evening Star
Twinkles on Grasmere no more,
But ruined and solemn and grey   20
The sheepfold of Michael survives;
And, far to the south, the heath
Still blows in the Quantock coombs,
By the favourite waters of Ruth.
These survive! – yet not without pain,
Pain and dejection to-night,
Can I feel that their poet is gone.

He grew old in an age he condemned.
He looked on the rushing decay
Of the times which had sheltered his youth;   30
Felt the dissolving throes
Of a social order he loved;
Outlived his brethren, his peers,

And, like the Theban seer,
Died in his enemies' day.

Cold bubbled the spring of Tilphusa,
Copais lay bright in the moon,
Helicon glassed in the lake
Its firs, and afar rose the peaks
Of Parnassus, snowily clear;   40
Thebes was behind him in flames,
And the clang of arms in his ear,
When his awe-struck captors led
The Theban seer to the spring.
Tiresias drank and died.
Nor did reviving Thebes
See such a prophet again.

Well may we mourn, when the head
Of a sacred poet lies low
In an age which can rear them no more!   50
The complaining millions of men
Darken in labour and pain;
But he was a priest to us all
Of the wonder and bloom of the world,
Which we saw with his eyes, and were glad.
He is dead, and the fruit-bearing day
Of his race is past on the earth;
And darkness returns to our eyes.

For, oh! is it you, is it you,
Moonlight, and shadow, and lake,   60
And mountains, that fill us with joy,
Or the poet who sings you so well?
Is it you, O beauty, O grace,
O charm, O romance, that we feel,
Or the voice which reveals what you are?
Are ye, like daylight and sun,
Shared and rejoiced in by all?

Or are ye immersed in the mass
Of matter, and hard to extract,
Or sunk at the core of the world   70
Too deep for the most to discern?
Like stars in the deep of the sky,
Which arise on the glass of the sage,
But are lost when their watcher is gone.

'They are here' – I heard, as men heard
In Mysian Ida the voice
Of the Mighty Mother, or Crete,
The murmur of Nature reply –
'Loveliness, magic, and grace,
They are here! they are set in the world,   80
They abide; and the finest of souls
Hath not been thrilled by them all,
Nor the dullest been dead to them quite.
The poet who sings them may die,
But they are immortal and live,
For they are the life of the world.
Will ye not learn it, and know,
When ye mourn that a poet is dead,
That the singer was less than his themes,
Life, and emotion, and I?   90

'More than the singer are these.
Weak is the tremor of pain
That thrills in his mournfullest chord
To that which once ran through his soul.
Cold the elation of joy
In his gladdest, airiest song,
To that which of old in his youth
Filled him and made him divine.
Hardly his voice at its best
Gives us a sense of the awe,   100
The vastness, the grandeur, the gloom
Of the unlit gulph of himself.

'Ye know not yourselves; and your bards –
The clearest, the best, who have read
Most in themselves – have beheld
Less than they left unrevealed.
Ye express not yourselves; can you make
With marble, with colour, with word,
What charmed you in others re-live?
Can thy pencil, O artist! restore   110
The figure, the bloom of thy love,
As she was in her morning of spring?
Canst thou paint the ineffable smile
Of her eyes as they rested on thine?
Can the image of life have the glow,
The motion of life itself?

'Yourselves and your fellows ye know not; and me,
The mateless, the one, will ye know?
Will ye scan me, and read me, and tell
Of the thoughts that ferment in my breast,   120
My longing, my sadness, my joy?
Will ye claim for your great ones the gift
To have rendered the gleam of my skies,
To have echoed the moan of my seas,
Uttered the voice of my hills?
When your great ones depart, will ye say:
All things have suffered a loss,
Nature is hid in their grave?

'Race after race, man after man,
Have thought that my secret was theirs,   130
Have dreamed that I lived but for them,
That they were my glory and joy.
– They are dust, they are changed, they are gone!
I remain.'

The Youth of Man

We, O Nature, depart,
Thou survivest us! this,
This, I know, is the law.
Yes! but more than this,
Thou who seest us die
Seest us change while we live;
Seest our dreams, one by one,
Seest our errors depart;
Watchest us, Nature! throughout,
Mild and inscrutably calm.   10

Well for us that we change!
Well for us that the power
Which in our morning-prime
Saw the mistakes of our youth,
Sweet, and forgiving, and good,
Sees the contrition of age!

  Behold, O Nature, this pair!
See them to-night where they stand,
Not with the halo of youth
Crowning their brows with its light,   20
Not with the sunshine of hope,
Not with the rapture of spring,
Which they had of old, when they stood
Years ago at my side
In this self-same garden, and said:
'We are young and the world is ours;
Man, man is the king of the world!
Fools that these mystics are
Who prate of Nature! for she
Hath neither beauty, nor warmth,   30
Nor life, nor emotion, nor power.
But man has a thousand gifts,
And the generous dreamer invests

The senseless world with them all.
Nature is nothing; her charm
Lives in our eyes which can paint,
Lives in our hearts which can feel.'

Thou, O Nature, wast mute,
Mute as of old! days flew,
Days and years; and Time   40
With the ceaseless stroke of his wings
Brushed off the bloom from their soul.
Clouded and dim grew their eye,
Languid their heart – for youth
Quickened its pulses no more.
Slowly, within the walls
Of an ever-narrowing world,
They drooped, they grew blind, they grew old.
Thee and their youth in thee,
Nature! they saw no more.   50

Murmur of living,
Stir of existence,
Soul of the world!
Make, oh, make yourselves felt
To the dying spirit of youth!
Come, like the breath of the spring!
Leave not a human soul
To grow old in darkness and pain!
Only the living can feel you,
But leave us not while we live!   60

Here they stand to-night –
Here, where this grey balustrade
Crowns the still valley; behind
Is the castled house, with its woods,
Which sheltered their childhood – the sun
On its ivied windows; a scent
From the grey-walled gardens, a breath

Of the fragrant stock and the pink,
Perfumes the evening air.
Their children play on the lawns.   70
They stand and listen; they hear
The children's shouts, and at times,
Faintly, the bark of a dog
From a distant farm in the hills.
Nothing besides! in front
The wide, wide valley outspreads
To the dim horizon, reposed
In the twilight, and bathed in dew,
Corn-field and hamlet and copse
Darkening fast; but a light,   80
Far off, a glory of day,
Still plays on the city spires;
And there in the dusk by the walls,
With the grey mist marking its course
Through the silent, flowery land,
On, to the plains, to the sea,
Floats the imperial stream.

   Well I know what they feel!
They gaze, and the evening wind
Plays on their faces; they gaze –   90
Airs from the Eden of youth
Awake and stir in their soul;
The past returns – they feel
What they are, alas! what they were.
They, not Nature, are changed.
Well I know what they feel!
Hush, for tears
Begin to steal to their eyes!
Hush, for fruit
Grows from such sorrow as theirs!   100

And they remember,
With piercing, untold anguish,

113

The proud boasting of their youth.
And they feel how Nature was fair.
And the mists of delusion,
And the scales of habit,
Fall away from their eyes;
And they see, for a moment,
Stretching out, like the desert
In its weary, unprofitable length,   110
Their faded, ignoble lives.

While the locks are yet brown on thy head,
While the soul still looks through thine eyes,
While the heart still pours
The mantling blood to thy cheek,
Sink, O youth, in thy soul!
Yearn to the greatness of Nature;
Rally the good in the depths of thyself!

A Summer Night

In the deserted, moon-blanched street,
How lonely rings the echo of my feet!
Those windows, which I gaze at, frown,
Silent and white, unopening down,
Repellent as the world; but see,
A break between the housetops shows
The moon! and, lost behind her, fading dim
Into the dewy dark obscurity
Down at the far horizon's rim,
Doth a whole tract of heaven disclose!   10

And to my mind the thought
Is on a sudden brought
Of a past night, and a far different scene.

Headlands stood out into the moonlit deep
As clearly as at noon;
The spring-tide's brimming flow
Heaved dazzlingly between;
Houses, with long white sweep,
Girdled the glistening bay;
Behind, through the soft air,   20
The blue haze-cradled mountains spread away.
That night was far more fair –
But the same restless pacings to and fro,
And the same vainly throbbing heart was there,
And the same bright, calm moon.

And the calm moonlight seems to say:
Hast thou then still the old unquiet breast,
Which neither deadens into rest,
Nor ever feels the fiery glow
That whirls the spirit from itself away,   30
But fluctuates to and fro,
Never by passion quite possessed
And never quite benumbed by the world's sway?
And I, I know not if to pray
Still to be what I am, or yield and be
Like all the other men I see.

For most men in a brazen prison live,
Where, in the sun's hot eye,
With heads bent o'er their toil, they languidly
Their lives to some unmeaning taskwork give,   40
Dreaming of nought beyond their prison-wall.
And as, year after year,
Fresh products of their barren labour fall
From their tired hands, and rest
Never yet comes more near,
Gloom settles slowly down over their breast;
And while they try to stem
The waves of mournful thought by which they are pressed,

Death in their prison reaches them,
Unfreed, having seen nothing, still unblest.   50

And the rest, a few,
Escape their prison and depart
On the wide ocean of life anew.
There the freed prisoner, where'er his heart
Listeth, will sail;
Nor doth he know how there prevail,
Despotic on that sea,
Trade-winds which cross it from eternity.
Awhile he holds some false way, undebarred
By thwarting signs, and braves   60
The freshening wind and blackening waves.
And then the tempest strikes him; and between
The lightning-bursts is seen
Only a driving wreck,
And the pale master on his spar-strewn deck
With anguished face and flying hair
Grasping the rudder hard,
Still bent to make some port he knows not where,
Still standing for some false, impossible shore.
And sterner comes the roar   70
Of sea and wind, and through the deepening gloom
Fainter and fainter wreck and helmsman loom,
And he too disappears, and comes no more.

Is there no life, but these alone?
Madman or slave, must man be one?
Plainness and clearness without shadow of stain!
Clearness divine!
Ye heavens, whose pure dark regions have no sign
Of languor, though so calm, and, though so great,
Are yet untroubled and unpassionate;   80
Who, though so noble, share in the world's toil,
And, though so tasked, keep free from dust and soil!
I will not say that your mild deeps retain

116

A tinge, it may be, of their silent pain
Who have longed deeply once, and longed in vain –
But I will rather say that you remain
A world above man's head, to let him see
How boundless might his soul's horizons be,
How vast, yet of what clear transparency!
How it were good to abide there, and breathe free;   90
How fair a lot to fill
Is left to each man still!

The Buried Life

Light flows our war of mocking words, and yet,
Behold, with tears mine eyes are wet!
I feel a nameless sadness o'er me roll.
Yes, yes, we know that we can jest,
We know, we know that we can smile!
But there's a something in this breast,
To which thy light words bring no rest,
And thy gay smiles no anodyne.
Give me thy hand, and hush awhile,
And turn those limpid eyes on mine,   10
And let me read there, love! thy inmost soul.

Alas! is even love too weak
To unlock the heart, and let it speak?
Are even lovers powerless to reveal
To one another what indeed they feel?
I knew the mass of men concealed
Their thoughts, for fear that if revealed
They would by other men be met
With blank indifference, or with blame reproved;
I knew they lived and moved   20
Tricked in disguises, alien to the rest

Of men, and alien to themselves – and yet
The same heart beats in every human breast!

But we, my love! – doth a like spell benumb
Our hearts, our voices? must we too be dumb?

Ah! well for us, if even we,
Even for a moment, can get free
Our heart, and have our lips unchained;
For that which seals them hath been deep-ordained!

Fate, which foresaw   30
How frivolous a baby man would be –
By what distractions he would be possessed.
How he would pour himself in every strife,
And well-nigh change his own identity –
That it might keep from his capricious play
His genuine self, and force him to obey
Even in his own despite his being's law,
Bade through the deep recesses of our breast
The unregarded river of our life
Pursue with indiscernible flow its way;   40
And that we should not see
The buried stream, and seem to be
Eddying at large in blind uncertainty,
Though driving on with it eternally.

But often, in the world's most crowded streets,
But often, in the din of strife,
There rises an unspeakable desire
After the knowledge of our buried life;
A thirst to spend our fire and restless force
In tracking out our true, original course;   50
A longing to inquire
Into the mystery of this heart which beats
So wild, so deep in us – to know
Whence our lives come and where they go.

And many a man in his own breast then delves,
But deep enough, alas! none ever mines.
And we have been on many thousand lines,
And we have shown, on each, spirit and power;
But hardly have we, for one little hour,
Been on our own line, have we been ourselves –   60
Hardly had skill to utter one of all
The nameless feelings that course through our breast,
But they course on for ever unexpressed.
And long we try in vain to speak and act
Our hidden self, and what we say and do
Is eloquent, is well – but 'tis not true!
And then we will no more be racked
With inward striving, and demand
Of all the thousand nothings of the hour
Their stupefying power;   70
Ah yes, and they benumb us at our call!
Yet still, from time to time, vague and forlorn,
From the soul's subterranean depth upborne
As from an infinitely distant land,
Come airs, and floating echoes, and convey
A melancholy into all our day.

Only – but this is rare –
When a belovéd hand is laid in ours,
When, jaded with the rush and glare
Of the interminable hours,   80
Our eyes can in another's eyes read clear,
When our world-deafened ear
Is by the tones of a loved voice caressed –
A bolt is shot back somewhere in our breast,
And a lost pulse of feeling stirs again.
The eye sinks inward, and the heart lies plain,
And what we mean, we say, and what we would, we know.
A man becomes aware of his life's flow,
And hears its winding murmur; and he sees
The meadows where it glides, the sun, the breeze.   90

And there arrives a lull in the hot race
Wherein he doth for ever chase
That flying and elusive shadow, rest.
An air of coolness plays upon his face,
And an unwonted calm pervades his breast.
And then he thinks he knows
The hills where his life rose,
And the sea where it goes.

Stanzas from the Grande Chartreuse

Through Alpine meadows soft-suffused
With rain, where thick the crocus blows,
Past the dark forges long disused,
The mule-track from Saint Laurent goes.
The bridge is crossed, and slow we ride,
Through forest, up the mountain-side.

The autumnal evening darkens round,
The wind is up, and drives the rain;
While, hark! far down, with strangled sound
Doth the Dead Guier's stream complain,   10
Where that wet smoke, among the woods,
Over his boiling cauldron broods.

Swift rush the spectral vapours white
Past limestone scars with ragged pines,
Showing – then blotting from our sight!
Halt – through the cloud-drift something shines!
High in the valley, wet and drear,
The huts of Courrerie appear.

Strike leftward! cries our guide; and higher
Mounts up the stony forest-way.   20

At last the encircling trees retire;
Look! through the showery twilight grey
What pointed roofs are these advance?
A palace of the Kings of France?

Approach, for what we seek is here!
Alight, and sparely sup, and wait
For rest in this outbuilding near;
Then cross the sward and reach that gate.
Knock; pass the wicket! Thou art come
To the Carthusians' world-famed home.   30

The silent courts, where night and day
Into their stone-carved basins cold
The splashing icy fountains play –
The humid corridors behold!
Where, ghostlike in the deepening night,
Cowled forms brush by in gleaming white.

The chapel, where no organ's peal
Invests the stern and naked prayer –
With penitential cries they kneel
And wrestle; rising then, with bare   40
And white uplifted faces stand,
Passing the Host from hand to hand;

Each takes, and then his visage wan
Is buried in his cowl once more.
The cells! – the suffering Son of Man
Upon the wall – the knee-worn floor –
And where they sleep, that wooden bed,
Which shall their coffin be, when dead!

The library, where tract and tome
Not to feed priestly pride are there,   50
To hymn the conquering march of Rome,
Nor yet to amuse, as ours are!

They paint of souls the inner strife,
Their drops of blood, their death in life.

The garden, overgrown – yet mild,
See, fragrant herbs are flowering there!
Strong children of the Alpine wild
Whose culture is the brethren's care;
Of human tasks their only one,
And cheerful works beneath the sun.   60

Those halls, too, destined to contain
Each its own pilgrim-host of old,
From England, Germany, or Spain –
All are before me! I behold
The House, the Brotherhood austere!
– And what am I, that I am here?

For rigorous teachers seized my youth,
And purged its faith, and trimmed its fire,
Showed me the high, white star of Truth,
There bade me gaze, and there aspire.   70
Even now their whispers pierce the gloom:
What dost thou in this living tomb?

Forgive me, masters of the mind!
At whose behest I long ago
So much unlearnt, so much resigned –
I come not here to be your foe!
I seek these anchorites, not in ruth,
To curse and to deny your truth;

Not as their friend, or child, I speak!
But as, on some far northern strand,   80
Thinking of his own Gods, a Greek
In pity and mournful awe might stand
Before some fallen Runic stone
For both were faiths, and both are gone.

Wandering between two worlds, one dead,
The other powerless to be born,
With nowhere yet to rest my head,
Like these, on earth I wait forlorn.
Their faith, my tears, the world deride –
I come to shed them at their side.   90

Oh, hide me in your gloom profound,
Ye solemn seats of holy pain!
Take me, cowled forms, and fence me round,
Till I possess my soul again;
Till free my thoughts before me roll,
Not chafed by hourly false control!

For the world cries your faith is now
But a dead time's exploded dream;
My melancholy, sciolists say,
Is a past mode, an outworn theme –   100
As if the world had ever had
A faith, or sciolists been sad!

Ah, if it *be* passed, take away,
At least, the restlessness, the pain;
Be man henceforth no more a prey
To these out-dated stings again!
The nobleness of grief is gone –
Ah, leave us not the fret alone!

But – if you cannot give us ease –
Last of the race of them who grieve,   110
Here leave us to die out with these
Last of the people who believe!
Silent, while years engrave the brow;
Silent – the best are silent now.

Achilles ponders in his tent,
The kings of modern thought are dumb;

Silent they are, though not content,
And wait to see the future come.
They have the grief men had of yore,
But they contend and cry no more. 120

Our fathers watered with their tears
This sea of time whereon we sail,
Their voices were in all men's ears
Who passed within their puissant hail.
Still the same ocean round us raves,
But we stand mute, and watch the waves.

For what availed it, all the noise
And outcry of the former men?
Say, have their sons achieved more joys,
Say, is life lighter now than then? 130
The sufferers died, they left their pain –
The pangs which tortured them remain.

What helps it now, that Byron bore,
With haughty scorn which mocked the smart,
Through Europe to the Ætolian shore
The pageant of his bleeding heart?
That thousands counted every groan,
And Europe made his woe her own?

What boots it, Shelley! that the breeze
Carried thy lovely wail away, 140
Musical through Italian trees
Which fringe thy soft blue Spezzian bay?
Inheritors of thy distress
Have restless hearts one throb the less?

Or are we easier, to have read,
O Obermann! the sad, stern page,
Which tells us how thou hidd'st thy head
From the fierce tempest of thine age

In the lone brakes of Fontainebleau,
Or chalets near the Alpine snow?   150

Ye slumber in your silent grave!
The world, which for an idle day
Grace to your mood of sadness gave,
Long since hath flung her weeds away.
The eternal trifler breaks your spell;
But we – we learnt your lore too well!

Years hence, perhaps, may dawn an age,
More fortunate, alas! than we,
Which without hardness will be sage,
And gay without frivolity.   160
Sons of the world, oh, speed those years;
But, while we wait, allow our tears!

Allow them! We admire with awe
The exulting thunder of your race;
You give the universe your law,
You triumph over time and space!
Your pride of life, your tireless powers,
We laud them, but they are not ours.

We are like children reared in shade
Beneath some old-world abbey wall,   170
Forgotten in a forest-glade,
And secret from the eyes of all.
Deep, deep the greenwood round them waves,
Their abbey, and its close of graves!

But, where the road runs near the stream,
Oft through the trees they catch a glance
Of passing troops in the sun's beam –
Pennon, and plume, and flashing lance!
Forth to the world those soldiers fare,
To life, to cities, and to war!   180

And through the wood, another way,
Faint bugle-notes from far are borne,
Where hunters gather, staghounds bay,
Round some fair forest-lodge at morn.
Gay dames are there, in sylvan green;
Laughter and cries – those notes between!

The banners flashing through the trees
Make their blood dance and chain their eyes;
That bugle-music on the breeze
Arrests them with a charmed surprise.   190
Banner by turns and bugle woo:
Ye shy recluses, follow too!

O children, what do ye reply? –
'Action and pleasure, will ye roam
Through these secluded dells to cry
And call us? – but too late ye come!
Too late for us your call ye blow,
Whose bent was taken long ago.

'Long since we pace this shadowed nave;
We watch those yellow tapers shine,   200
Emblems of hope over the grave,
In the high altar's depth divine;
The organ carries to our ear
Its accents of another sphere.

'Fenced early in this cloistral round
Of reverie, of shade, of prayer,
How should we grow in other ground?
How can we flower in foreign air?
– Pass, banners, pass, and bugles, cease;
And leave our desert to its peace!'   210

The Tomb

So rest, for ever rest, O princely Pair!
In your high church, 'mid the still mountain-air,
Where horn, and hound, and vassals, never come.
Only the blessed Saints are smiling dumb,
From the rich painted windows of the nave,
On aisle, and transept, and your marble grave;
Where thou, young Prince! shalt never more arise
From the fringed mattress where thy Duchess lies,
On autumn-mornings, when the bugle sounds,
And ride across the drawbridge with thy hounds   10
To hunt the boar in the crisp woods till eve;
And thou, O Princess! shalt no more receive,
Thou and thy ladies, in the hall of state,
The jaded hunters with their bloody freight,
Coming benighted to the castle-gate.

  So sleep, for ever sleep, O marble Pair!
Or, if ye wake, let it be then, when fair
On the carved western front a flood of light
Streams from the setting sun, and colours bright
Prophets, transfigured Saints, and Martyrs brave,   20
In the vast western window of the nave;
And on the pavement round the Tomb there glints
A chequer-work of glowing sapphire-tints,
And amethyst, and ruby – then unclose
Your eyelids on the stone where ye repose,
And from your broidered pillows lift your heads,
And rise upon your cold white marble beds;
And, looking down on the warm rosy tints,
Which chequer, at your feet, the illumined flints,
Say: *What is this? we are in bliss – forgiven –*   30
Behold the pavement of the courts of Heaven!
Or let it be on autumn nights, when rain
Doth rustlingly above your heads complain
On the smooth leaden roof, and on the walls
Shedding her pensive light at intervals

127

The moon through the clere-story windows shines,
And the wind washes through the mountain-pines.
Then, gazing up 'mid the dim pillars high,
The foliaged marble forest where ye lie,
Hush, ye will say, *it is eternity!*   40
This is the glimmering verge of Heaven, and these
The columns of the heavenly palaces!
And, in the sweeping of the wind, your ear
The passage of the Angels' wings will hear,
And on the lichen-crusted leads above
The rustle of the eternal rain of love.

Sohrab and Rustum

AN EPISODE

And the first grey of morning filled the east,
And the fog rose out of the Oxus stream.
But all the Tartar camp along the stream
Was hushed, and still the men were plunged in sleep;
Sohrab alone, he slept not; all night long
He had lain wakeful, tossing on his bed;
But when the grey dawn stole into his tent,
He rose, and clad himself, and girt his sword,
And took his horseman's cloak, and left his tent,
And went abroad into the cold wet fog,   10
Through the dim camp to Peran-Wisa's tent.
   Through the black Tartar tents he passed, which stood
Clustering like bee-hives on the low flat strand
Of Oxus, where the summer-floods o'erflow
When the sun melts the snows in high Pamere;
Through the black tents he passed, o'er that low strand
And to a hillock came, a little back
From the stream's brink – the spot where first a boat,

Crossing the stream in summer, scrapes the land.
The men of former times had crowned the top 20
With a clay fort; but that was fallen, and now
The Tartars built there Peran-Wisa's tent,
A dome of laths, and o'er it felts were spread.
And Sohrab came there, and went in, and stood
Upon the thick piled carpets in the tent,
And found the old man sleeping on his bed
Of rugs and felts, and near him lay his arms.
And Peran-Wisa heard him, though the step
Was dulled; for he slept light, an old man's sleep;
And he rose quickly on one arm, and said:– 30

'Who art thou? for it is not yet clear dawn.
Speak! is there news, or any night alarm?'
    But Sohrab came to the bedside, and said:–
'Thou know'st me, Peran-Wisa! it is I.
The sun is not yet risen, and the foe
Sleep; but I sleep not; all night long I lie
Tossing and wakeful, and I come to thee.
For so did King Afrasiab bid me seek
Thy counsel, and to heed thee as thy son,
In Samarcand, before the army marched; 40
And I will tell thee what my heart desires.
Thou know'st if, since from Ader-baijan first
I came among the Tartars and bore arms,
I have still served Afrasiab well, and shown,
At my boy's years, the courage of a man.
This too thou know'st, that while I still bear on
The conquering Tartar ensigns through the world,
And beat the Persians back on every field,
I seek one man, one man, and one alone –
Rustum, my father; who I hoped should greet, 50
Should one day greet, upon some well-fought field,
His not unworthy, not inglorious son.
So I long hoped, but him I never find.
Come then, hear now, and grant me what I ask.
Let the two armies rest to-day; but I

Will challenge forth the bravest Persian lords
To meet me, man to man; if I prevail,
Rustum will surely hear it; if I fall –
Old man, the dead need no one, claim no kin.
Dim is the rumour of a common fight, 60
Where host meets host, and many names are sunk;
But of a single combat fame speaks clear.'
    He spoke; and Peran-Wisa took the hand
Of the young man in his, and sighed, and said:–
    'O Sohrab, an unquiet heart is thine!
Canst thou not rest among the Tartar chiefs,
And share the battle's common chance with us
Who love thee, but must press for ever first,
In single fight incurring single risk,
To find a father thou hast never seen? 70
That were far best, my son, to stay with us
Unmurmuring; in our tents, while it is war,
And when 'tis truce, then in Afrasiab's towns.
But, if this one desire indeed rules all,
To seek out Rustum – seek him not through fight!
Seek him in peace, and carry to his arms,
O Sohrab, carry an unwounded son!
But far hence seek him, for he is not here.
For now it is not as when I was young,
When Rustum was in front of every fray; 80
But now he keeps apart, and sits at home,
In Seistan, with Zal, his father old.
Whether that his own mighty strength at last
Feels the abhorred approaches of old age,
Or in some quarrel with the Persian King.
There go! – Thou wilt not? Yet my heart forbodes
Danger or death awaits thee on this field.
Fain would I know thee safe and well, though lost
To us; fain therefore send thee hence, in peace
To seek thy father, not seek single fights 90
In vain; but who can keep the lion's cub
From ravening, and who govern Rustum's son?

Go, I will grant thee what thy heart desires.'
   So said he, and dropped Sohrab's hand, and left
His bed, and the warm rugs whereon he lay;
And o'er his chilly limbs his woollen coat
He passed, and tied his sandals on his feet,
And threw a white cloak round him, and he took
In his right hand a ruler's staff, no sword;
And on his head he set his sheep-skin cap,   100
Black, glossy, curled, the fleece of Kara-Kul;
And raised the curtain of his tent, and called
His herald to his side, and went abroad.

   The sun by this had risen, and cleared the fog
From the broad Oxus and the glittering sands.
And from their tents the Tartar horsemen filed
Into the open plain; so Haman bade –
Haman, who next to Peran-Wisa ruled
The host, and still was in his lusty prime.
From their black tents, long files of horse, they streamed; 110
As when some grey November morn the files,
In marching order spread, of long-necked cranes
Stream over Casbin and the southern slopes
Of Elburz, from the Aralian estuaries,
Or some frore Caspian reed-bed, southward bound
For the warm Persian sea-board – so they streamed.
The Tartars of the Oxus, the King's guard,
First, with black sheep-skin caps and with long spears;
Large men, large steeds; who from Bokhara come
And Khiva, and ferment the milk of mares.   120
Next, the more temperate Toorkmuns of the south,
The Tukas, and the lances of Salore,
And those from Attruck and the Caspian sands;
Light men and on light steeds, who only drink
The acrid milk of camels, and their wells.
And then a swarm of wandering horse, who came
From far, and a more doubtful service owned;
The Tartars of Ferghana, from the banks
Of the Jaxartes, men with scanty beards

And close-set skull-caps; and those wilder hordes 130
Who roam o'er Kipchak and the northern waste,
Kalmucks and unkempt Kuzzaks, tribes who stray
Nearest the Pole, and wandering Kirghizzes,
Who come on shaggy ponies from Pamere;
These all filed out from camp into the plain.
And on the other side the Persians formed;
First a light cloud of horse, Tartars they seemed,
The Ilyats of Khorassan; and behind,
The royal troops of Persia, horse and foot,
Marshalled battalions bright in burnished steel. 140
But Peran-Wisa with his herald came,
Threading the Tartar squadrons to the front,
And with his staff kept back the foremost ranks.
And when Ferood, who led the Persians, saw
That Peran-Wisa kept the Tartars back,
He took his spear, and to the front he came,
And checked his ranks, and fixed them where they stood.
And the old Tartar came upon the sand
Betwixt the silent hosts, and spake, and said:–
   'Ferood, and ye, Persians and Tartars, hear! 150
Let there be truce between the hosts to-day.
But choose a champion from the Persian lords
To fight our champion Sohrab, man to man.'
   As, in the country, on a morn in June,
When the dew glistens on the pearléd ears,
A shiver runs through the deep corn for joy –
So, when they heard what Peran-Wisa said,
A thrill through all the Tartar squadrons ran
Of pride and hope for Sohrab, whom they loved.
   But as a troop of pedlars, from Cabool, 160
Cross underneath the Indian Caucasus,
That vast sky-neighbouring mountain of milk snow;
Crossing so high, that, as they mount, they pass
Long flocks of travelling birds dead on the snow,
Choked by the air, and scarce can they themselves
Slake their parched throats with sugared mulberries –

In single file they move, and stop their breath,
For fear they should dislodge the o'erhanging snows –
So the pale Persians held their breath with fear.

   And to Ferood his brother chiefs came up   170
To counsel; Gudurz and Zoarrah came,
And Feraburz, who ruled the Persian host
Second, and was the uncle of the King;
These came and counselled, and then Gudurz said:–

   'Ferood, shame bids us take their challenge up,
Yet champion have we none to match this youth.
He has the wild stag's foot, the lion's heart.
But Rustum came last night; aloof he sits
And sullen, and has pitched his tents apart.
Him will I seek, and carry to his ear   180
The Tartar challenge, and this young man's name.
Haply he will forget his wrath, and fight.
Stand forth the while, and take their challenge up.'

   So spake he; and Ferood stood forth and cried:–
'Old man, be it agreed as thou hast said!
Let Sohrab arm, and we will find a man.'

   He spake: and Peran-Wisa turned, and strode
Back through the opening squadrons to his tent.
But through the anxious Persians Gudurz ran,
And crossed the camp which lay behind, and reached,   190
Out on the sands beyond it, Rustum's tents.
Of scarlet cloth they were, and glittering gay,
Just pitched; the high pavilion in the midst
Was Rustum's, and his men lay camped around.
And Gudurz entered Rustum's tent, and found
Rustum; his morning meal was done, but still
The table stood before him, charged with food –
A side of roasted sheep, and cakes of bread,
And dark green melons; and there Rustum sate
Listless, and held a falcon on his wrist,   200
And played with it; but Gudurz came and stood
Before him; and he looked, and saw him stand,
And with a cry sprang up and dropped the bird,

And greeted Gudurz with both hands, and said:–
   'Welcome! these eyes could see no better sight.
What news? but sit down first, and eat and drink.'
   But Gudurz stood in the tent-door, and said:–
'Not now! a time will come to eat and drink,
But not to-day; to-day has other needs.
The armies are drawn out, and stand at gaze;   210
For from the Tartars is a challenge brought
To pick a champion from the Persian lords
To fight their champion – and thou know'st his name –
Sohrab men call him, but his birth is hid.
O Rustum, like thy might is this young man's!
He has the wild stag's foot, the lion's heart;
And he is young, and Iran's chiefs are old,
Or else too weak; and all eyes turn to thee.
Come down and help us, Rustum, or we lose!'
   He spoke, but Rustum answered with a smile:–   220
'Go to! if Iran's chiefs are old, then I
Am older; if the young are weak, the King
Errs strangely; for the King, for Kai Khosroo,
Himself is young, and honours younger men,
And lets the agéd moulder to their graves.
Rustum he loves no more, but loves the young –
The young may rise at Sohrab's vaunts, not I.
For what care I, though all speak Sohrab's fame?
For would that I myself had such a son,
And not that one slight helpless girl I have –   230
A son so famed, so brave, to send to war,
And I to tarry with the snow-haired Zal,
My father, whom the robber Afghans vex,
And clip his borders short, and drive his herds,
And he has none to guard his weak old age.
There would I go, and hang my armour up,
And with my great name fence that weak old man,
And spend the goodly treasures I have got,
And rest my age, and hear of Sohrab's fame,
And leave to death the hosts of thankless kings,   240

134

And with these slaughterous hands draw sword no more.'
   He spoke, and smiled; and Gudurz made reply:–
'What then, O Rustum, will men say to this,
When Sohrab dares our bravest forth, and seeks
Thee most of all, and thou, whom most he seeks,
Hidest thy face? Take heed lest men should say:
Like some old miser, Rustum hoards his fame,
And shuns to peril it with younger men.'
   And, greatly moved, then Rustum made reply:–   250
'O Gudurz, wherefore dost thou say such words?
Thou knowest better words than this to say.
What is one more, one less, obscure or famed,
Valiant or craven, young or old, to me?
Are they not mortal, am not I myself?
But who for men of nought would do great deeds?
Come, thou shalt see how Rustum hoards his fame!
But I will fight unknown, and in plain arms;
Let not men say of Rustum, he was matched
In single fight with any mortal man.'
   He spoke, and frowned; and Gudurz turned, and ran   260
Back quickly through the camp in fear and joy –
Fear at his wrath, but joy that Rustum came.
But Rustum strode to his tent-door, and called
His followers in, and bade them bring his arms,
And clad himself in steel; the arms he chose
Were plain, and on his shield was no device,
Only his helm was rich, inlaid with gold,
And, from the fluted spine atop, a plume
Of horsehair waved, a scarlet horsehair plume.
So armed, he issued forth; and Ruksh, his horse,   270
Followed him like a faithful hound at heel –
Ruksh, whose renown was noised through all the earth,
The horse, whom Rustum on a foray once
Did in Bokhara by the river find
A colt beneath its dam, and drove him home,
And reared him; a bright bay, with lofty crest,
Dight with a saddle-cloth of broidered green

135

Crusted with gold, and on the ground were worked
All beasts of chase, all beasts which hunters know.
So followed, Rustum left his tents, and crossed   280
The camp, and to the Persian host appeared.
And all the Persians knew him, and with shouts
Hailed; but the Tartars knew not who he was.
And dear as the wet diver to the eyes
Of his pale wife who waits and weeps on shore,
By sandy Bahrein, in the Persian Gulf,
Plunging all day in the blue waves, at night,
Having made up his tale of precious pearls,
Rejoins her in their hut upon the sands –
So dear to the pale Persians Rustum came.   290
    And Rustum to the Persian front advanced,
And Sohrab armed in Haman's tent, and came.
And as afield the reapers cut a swath
Down through the middle of a rich man's corn,
And on each side are squares of standing corn,
And in the midst a stubble, short and bare –
So on each side were squares of men, with spears
Bristling, and in the midst, the open sand.
And Rustum came upon the sand, and cast
His eyes toward the Tartar tents, and saw   300
Sohrab come forth, and eyed him as he came.
    As some rich woman, on a winter's morn,
Eyes through her silken curtains the poor drudge
Who with numb blackened fingers makes her fire –
At cock-crow, on a starlit winter's morn,
When the frost flowers the whitened window-panes –
And wonders how she lives, and what the thoughts
Of that poor drudge may be; so Rustum eyed
The unknown adventurous youth, who from afar
Came seeking Rustum, and defying forth   310
All the most valiant chiefs; long he perused
His spirited air, and wondered who he was.
For very young he seemed, tenderly reared;
Like some young cypress, tall, and dark, and straight,

Which in a queen's secluded garden throws
Its slight dark shadow on the moonlit turf,
By midnight, to a bubbling fountain's sound –
So slender Sohrab seemed, so softly reared.
And a deep pity entered Rustum's soul
As he beheld him coming; and he stood,   320
And beckoned to him with his hand, and said:–

  'O thou young man, the air of Heaven is soft,
And warm, and pleasant; but the grave is cold!
Heaven's air is better than the cold dead grave.
Behold me! I am vast, and clad in iron,
And tried; and I have stood on many a field
Of blood, and I have fought with many a foe –
Never was that field lost, or that foe saved.
O Sohrab, wherefore wilt thou rush on death?
Be governed! quit the Tartar host, and come   330
To Iran, and be as my son to me,
And fight beneath my banner till I die!
There are no youths in Iran brave as thou.'

  So he spake, mildly; Sohrab heard his voice,
The mighty voice of Rustum, and he saw
His giant figure planted on the sand,
Sole, like some single tower, which a chief
Hath builded on the waste in former years
Against the robbers; and he saw that head,
Streaked with its first grey hairs; hope filled his soul,   340
And he ran forward and embraced his knees,
And clasped his hand within his own, and said:–

  'O, by my father's head! by thine own soul!
Art thou not Rustum? speak! art thou not he?'

  But Rustum eyed askance the kneeling youth,
And turned away, and spake to his own soul:–

  'Ah me, I muse what this young fox may mean!
False, wily, boastful, are these Tartar boys.
For if I now confess this thing he asks,
And hide it not, but say: *Rustum is here!*   350
He will not yield indeed, nor quit our foes,

137

But he will find some pretext not to fight,
And praise my fame, and proffer courteous gifts,
A belt or sword perhaps, and go his way.
And on a feast-side, in Afrasiab's hall,
In Samarcand, he will arise and cry:
"I challenged once, when the two armies camped
Beside the Oxus, all the Persian lords
To cope with me in single fight; but they
Shrank, only Rustum dared; then he and I   360
Changed gifts, and went on equal terms away."
So will he speak, perhaps, while men applaud;
Then were the chiefs of Iran shamed through me.'
   And then he turned, and sternly spake aloud:–
'Rise! wherefore dost thou vainly question thus
Of Rustum? I am here, whom thou hast called
By challenge forth; make good thy vaunt, or yield!
Is it with Rustum only thou wouldst fight?
Rash boy, men look on Rustum's face and flee!
For well I know, that did great Rustum stand   370
Before thy face this day, and were revealed,
There would be then no talk of fighting more.
But being what I am, I tell thee this –
Do thou record it in thine inmost soul:
Either thou shalt renounce thy vaunt and yield,
Or else thy bones shall strew this sand, till winds
Bleach them, or Oxus with his summer floods,
Oxus in summer wash them all away.'
   He spoke; and Sohrab answered, on his feet:–
'Art thou so fierce? Thou wilt not fright me so!   380
I am no girl, to be made pale by words.
Yet this thou hast said well, did Rustum stand
Here on this field, there were no fighting then.
But Rustum is far hence, and we stand here.
Begin! thou art more vast, more dread than I,
And thou art proved, I know, and I am young –
But yet success sways with the breath of Heaven.
And though thou thinkest that thou knowest sure

Thy victory, yet thou canst not surely know.
For we are all, like swimmers in the sea,   390
Poised on the top of a huge wave of fate,
Which hangs uncertain to which side to fall.
And whether it will heave us up to land,
Or whether it will roll us out to sea,
Back out to sea, to the deep waves of death,
We know not, and no search will make us know;
Only the event will teach us in its hour.'
    He spoke, and Rustum answered not, but hurled
His spear; down from the shoulder, down it came,
As on some partridge in the corn a hawk,   400
That long has towered in the airy clouds,
Drops like a plummet; Sohrab saw it come,
And sprang aside, quick as a flash; the spear
Hissed, and went quivering down into the sand,
Which it sent flying wide; then Sohrab threw
In turn, and full struck Rustum's shield; sharp rang,
The iron plates rang sharp, but turned the spear.
And Rustum seized his club, which none but he
Could wield; an unlopped trunk it was, and huge,
Still rough – like those which men in treeless plains   410
To build them boats fish from the flooded rivers,
Hyphasis or Hydaspes, when, high up
By their dark springs, the wind in winter-time
Hath made in Himalayan forests wrack,
And strewn the channels with torn boughs – so huge
The club which Rustum lifted now, and struck
One stroke; but again Sohrab sprang aside,
Lithe as the glancing snake, and the club came
Thundering to earth, and leapt from Rustum's hand.
And Rustum followed his own blow, and fell   420
To his knees, and with his fingers clutched the sand;
And now might Sohrab have unsheathed his sword,
And pierced the mighty Rustum while he lay
Dizzy, and on his knees, and choked with sand;
But he looked on, and smiled, nor bared his sword,

But courteously drew back, and spoke, and said:–
  'Thou strik'st too hard! that club of thine will float
Upon the summer-floods, and not my bones.
But rise, and be not wroth! not wroth am I;
No, when I see thee, wrath forsakes my soul.   430
Thou say'st, thou art not Rustum; be it so!
Who art thou then, that canst so touch my soul?
Boy as I am, I have seen battles too –
Have waded foremost in their bloody waves,
And heard their hollow roar of dying men;
But never was my heart thus touched before.
Are they from Heaven, these softenings of the heart?
O thou old warrior, let us yield to Heaven!
Come, plant we here in earth our angry spears,
And make a truce, and sit upon this sand,   440
And pledge each other in red wine, like friends,
And thou shalt talk to me of Rustum's deeds.
There are enough foes in the Persian host,
Whom I may meet, and strike, and feel no pang;
Champions enough Afrasiab has, whom thou
Mayst fight; fight *them*, when they confront thy spear!
But oh, let there be peace 'twixt thee and me!'
  He ceased, but while he spake, Rustum had risen,
And stood erect, trembling with rage; his club
He left to lie, but had regained his spear,   450
Whose fiery point now in his mailed right-hand
Blazed bright and baleful, like that autumn-star,
The baleful sign of fevers; dust had soiled
His stately crest, and dimmed his glittering arms.
His breast heaved, his lips foamed, and twice his voice
Was choked with rage; at last these words broke way:–
  'Girl! nimble with thy feet, not with thy hands!
Curled minion, dancer, coiner of sweet words!
Fight, let me hear thy hateful voice no more!
Thou art not in Afrasiab's gardens now   460
With Tartar girls, with whom thou art wont to dance;
But on the Oxus-sands, and in the dance

140

Of battle, and with me, who make no play
Of war; I fight it out, and hand to hand.
Speak not to me of truce, and pledge, and wine!
Remember all thy valour; try thy feints
And cunning! all the pity I had is gone;
Because thou hast shamed me before both the hosts
With thy light skipping tricks, and thy girl's wiles.'

He spoke, and Sohrab kindled at his taunts,   470
And he too drew his sword; at once they rushed
Together, as two eagles on one prey
Come rushing down together from the clouds,
One from the east, one from the west; their shields
Dashed with a clang together, and a din
Rose, such as that the sinewy woodcutters
Make often in the forest's heart at morn,
Of hewing axes, crashing trees – such blows
Rustum and Sohrab on each other hailed.
And you would say that sun and stars took part   480
In that unnatural conflict; for a cloud
Grew suddenly in Heaven, and darked the sun
Over the fighters' heads; and a wind rose
Under their feet, and moaning swept the plain,
And in a sandy whirlwind wrapped the pair.
In gloom they twain were wrapped, and they alone;
For both the on-looking hosts on either hand
Stood in broad daylight, and the sky was pure,
And the sun sparkled on the Oxus stream.
But in the gloom they fought, with bloodshot eyes   490
And labouring breath; first Rustum struck the shield
Which Sohrab held stiff out; the steel-spiked spear
Rent the tough plates, but failed to reach the skin,
And Rustum plucked it back with angry groan.
Then Sohrab with his sword smote Rustum's helm,
Nor clove its steel quite through; but all the crest
He shore away, and that proud horsehair plume,
Never till now defiled, sank to the dust;
And Rustum bowed his head; but then the gloom

Grew blacker, thunder rumbled in the air,   500
And lightnings rent the cloud; and Ruksh, the horse,
Who stood at hand, uttered a dreadful cry;
No horse's cry was that, most like the roar
Of some pained desert-lion, who all day
Hath trailed the hunter's javelin in his side,
And comes at night to die upon the sand.
The two hosts heard that cry, and quaked for fear,
And Oxus curdled as it crossed his stream.
But Sohrab heard, and quailed not, but rushed on,
And struck again; and again Rustum bowed   510
His head; but this time all the blade, like glass,
Sprang in a thousand shivers on the helm,
And in the hand the hilt remained alone.
Then Rustum raised his head; his dreadful eyes
Glared, and he shook on high his menacing spear,
And shouted: *Rustum!* – Sohrab heard that shout,
And shrank amazed; back he recoiled one step,
And scanned with blinking eyes the advancing form;
And then he stood bewildered; and he dropped
His covering shield, and the spear pierced his side.   520
He reeled, and staggering back, sank to the ground;
And then the gloom dispersed, and the wind fell,
And the bright sun broke forth, and melted all
The cloud; and the two armies saw the pair –
Saw Rustum standing, safe upon his feet,
And Sohrab, wounded, on the bloody sand.
    Then, with a bitter smile, Rustum began:–
'Sohrab, thou thoughtest in thy mind to kill
A Persian lord this day, and strip his corpse,
And bear thy trophies to Afrasiab's tent.   530
Or else that the great Rustum would come down
Himself to fight, and that thy wiles would move
His heart to take a gift, and let thee go.
And then that all the Tartar host would praise
Thy courage or thy craft, and spread thy fame,
To glad thy father in his weak old age.

142

Fool, thou art slain, and by an unknown man!
Dearer to the red jackals shalt thou be
Than to thy friends, and to thy father old.'
    And, with a fearless mien, Sohrab replied:—   540
'Unknown thou art; yet thy fierce vaunt is vain.
Thou dost not slay me, proud and boastful man!
No! Rustum slays me, and this filial heart.
For were I matched with ten such men as thee,
And I were that which till to-day I was,
They should be lying here, I standing there.
But that belovéd name unnerved my arm –
That name, and something, I confess, in thee,
Which troubles all my heart, and made my shield
Fall; and thy spear transfixed an unarmed foe.   550
And now thou boastest, and insult'st my fate.
But hear thou this, fierce man, tremble to hear:
The mighty Rustum shall avenge my death!
My father, whom I seek through all the world,
He shall avenge my death, and punish thee!'
    As when some hunter in the spring hath found
A breeding eagle sitting on her nest,
Upon the craggy isle of a hill-lake,
And pierced her with an arrow as she rose,
And followed her to find her where she fell   560
Far off; anon her mate comes winging back
From hunting, and a great way off descries
His huddling young left sole; at that, he checks
His pinion, and with short uneasy sweeps
Circles above his eyry, with loud screams
Chiding his mate back to her nest; but she
Lies dying, with the arrow in her side,
In some far stony gorge out of his ken,
A heap of fluttering feathers – never more
Shall the lake glass her, flying over it;   570
Never the black and dripping precipices
Echo her stormy scream as she sails by –
As that poor bird flies home, nor knows his loss,

143

So Rustum knew not his own loss, but stood
Over his dying son, and knew him not.
    But, with a cold incredulous voice, he said:–
'What prate is this of fathers and revenge?
The mighty Rustum never had a son.'
    And, with a failing voice, Sohrab replied:–
'Ah yes, he had! and that lost son am I.   580
Surely the news will one day reach his ear,
Reach Rustum, where he sits, and tarries long,
Somewhere, I know not where, but far from here;
And pierce him like a stab, and make him leap
To arms, and cry for vengeance upon thee.
Fierce man, bethink thee, for an only son!
What will that grief, what will that vengeance be?
Oh, could I live, till I that grief had seen!
Yet him I pity not so much, but her,
My mother, who in Ader-baijan dwells   590
With that old king, her father, who grows grey
With age, and rules over the valiant Koords.
Her most I pity, who no more will see
Sohrab returning from the Tartar camp,
With spoils and honour, when the war is done.
But a dark rumour will be bruited up,
From tribe to tribe, until it reach her ear;
And then will that defenceless woman learn
That Sohrab will rejoice her sight no more,
But that in battle with a nameless foe,   600
By the far-distant Oxus, he is slain.'
    He spoke; and as he ceased, he wept aloud,
Thinking of her he left, and his own death.
He spoke; but Rustum listened, plunged in thought.
Nor did he yet believe it was his son
Who spoke, although he called back names he knew;
For he had had sure tidings that the babe,
Which was in Ader-baijan born to him,
Had been a puny girl, no boy at all –
So that sad mother sent him word, for fear   610

Rustum should seek the boy, to train in arms.
And so he deemed that either Sohrab took,
By a false boast, the style of Rustum's son;
Or that men gave it him, to swell his fame.
So deemed he; yet he listened, plunged in thought:
And his soul set to grief, as the vast tide
Of the bright rocking Ocean sets to shore
At the full moon; tears gathered in his eyes;
For he remembered his own early youth,
And all its bounding rapture; as, at dawn,   620
The shepherd from his mountain-lodge descries
A far, bright city, smitten by the sun,
Through many rolling clouds – so Rustum saw
His youth; saw Sohrab's mother, in her bloom;
And that old king, her father, who loved well
His wandering guest, and gave him his fair child
With joy; and all the pleasant life they led,
They three, in that long-distant summer-time –
The castle, and the dewy woods, and hunt
And hound, and morn on those delightful hills   630
In Ader-baijan. And he saw that Youth,
Of age and looks to be his own dear son,
Piteous and lovely, lying on the sand,
Like some rich hyacinth which by the scythe
Of an unskilful gardener has been cut,
Mowing the garden grass-plots near its bed,
And lies, a fragrant tower of purple bloom,
On the mown, dying grass – so Sohrab lay,
Lovely in death, upon the common sand.
And Rustum gazed on him with grief, and said:–   640
    'O Sohrab, thou indeed art such a son
Whom Rustum, wert thou his, might well have loved.
Yet here thou errest, Sohrab, or else men
Have told thee false – thou art not Rustum's son.
For Rustum had no son; one child he had –
But one – a girl; who with her mother now
Plies some light female task, nor dreams of us –

Of us she dreams not, nor of wounds, nor war.'
    But Sohrab answered him in wrath; for now
The anguish of the deep-fixed spear grew fierce,   650
And he desired to draw forth the steel,
And let the blood flow free, and so to die –
But first he would convince his stubborn foe;
And, rising sternly on one arm, he said:–
    'Man, who art thou who dost deny my words?
Truth sits upon the lips of dying men,
And falsehood, while I lived, was far from mine.
I tell thee, pricked upon this arm I bear
That seal which Rustum to my mother gave,
That she might prick it on the babe she bore.'   660
    He spoke; and all the blood left Rustum's cheeks,
And his knees tottered, and he smote his hand
Against his breast, his heavy mailéd hand,
That the hard iron corslet clanked aloud;
And to his heart he pressed the other hand,
And in a hollow voice he spake, and said:–
    'Sohrab, that were a proof which could not lie!
If thou show this, then art thou Rustum's son.'
    Then, with weak hasty fingers, Sohrab loosed
His belt, and near the shoulder bared his arm,   670
And showed a sign in faint vermilion points
Pricked; as a cunning workman, in Pekin,
Pricks with vermilion some clear porcelain vase,
An emperor's gift – at early morn he paints,
And all day long, and, when night comes, the lamp
Lights up his studious forehead and thin hands –
So delicately pricked the sign appeared
On Sohrab's arm, the sign of Rustum's seal.
It was that griffin, which of old reared Zal,
Rustum's great father, whom they left to die,   680
A helpless babe, among the mountain-rocks;
Him that kind creature found, and reared, and loved –
And Sohrab bared that image on his arm,
And himself scanned it long with mournful eyes,

146

And then he touched it with his hand and said:–
  'How say'st thou! Is that sign the proper sign
Of Rustum's son, or of some other man's?'
  He spoke; but Rustum gazed, and gazed, and stood
Speechless; and then he uttered one sharp cry:
O boy – thy father! – and his voice choked there.   690
And then a dark cloud passed before his eyes,
And his head swam, and he sank down to earth.
But Sohrab crawled to where he lay, and cast
His arms about his neck, and kissed his lips,
And with fond faltering fingers stroked his cheeks,
Trying to call him back to life; and life
Came back to Rustum, and he oped his eyes,
And they stood wide with horror; and he seized
In both his hands the dust which lay around,
And threw it on his head, and smirched his hair,   700
His hair, and face, and beard, and glittering arms;
And strong convulsive groanings shook his breast,
And his sobs choked him; and he clutched his sword,
To draw it, and for ever let life out.
But Sohrab saw his thought, and held his hands,
And with a soothing voice he spake, and said:–
  'Father, forbear! for I but meet to-day
The doom which at my birth was written down
In Heaven, and thou art Heaven's unconscious hand.
Surely my heart cried out that it was thou,   710
When first I saw thee; and thy heart spoke too,
I know it! but fate trod those promptings down
Under its iron heel; fate, fate engaged
The strife, and hurled me on my father's spear.
But let us speak no more of this! I find
My father; let me feel that I have found!
Come, sit beside me on this sand, and take
My head betwixt thy hands, and kiss my cheeks,
And wash them with thy tears, and say: *My son!*
Quick! quick! for numbered are my sands of life,   720
And swift; for like the lightning to this field

147

I came, and like the wind I go away –
Sudden, and swift, and like a passing wind.
But it was writ in Heaven that this should be.'
    So said he, and his voice released the heart
Of Rustum, and his tears broke forth; he cast
His arm round his son's neck, and wept aloud,
And kissed him. And awe fell on both the hosts,
When they saw Rustum's grief; and Ruksh, the horse,
With his head bowing to the ground and mane   730
Sweeping the dust, came near, and in mute woe
First to the one then to the other moved
His head, as if inquiring what their grief
Might mean; and from his dark, compassionate eyes,
The big warm tears rolled down, and caked the sand.
But Rustum chid him with stern voice, and said:–
    'Ruksh, now thou grievest; but, O Ruksh, thy feet
Should first have rotted on their nimble joints,
Or ere they brought thy master to this field!'
    But Sohrab looked upon the horse and said:–   740
'Is this, then, Ruksh? How often, in past days,
My mother told me of thee, thou brave steed,
My terrible father's terrible horse! and said,
That I should one day find thy lord and thee.
Come, let me lay my hand upon thy mane!
O Ruksh, thou art more fortunate than I;
For thou hast gone where I shall never go,
And snuffed the breezes of my father's home.
And thou hast trod the sands of Seistan,
And seen the River of Helmund, and the Lake   750
Of Zirrah; and the aged Zal himself
Has often stroked thy neck, and given thee food,
Corn in a golden platter soaked with wine,
And said: *O Ruksh! bear Rustum well!* – but I
Have never known my grandsire's furrowed face,
Nor seen his lofty house in Seistan,
Nor slaked my thirst at the clear Helmund stream;
But lodged among my father's foes, and seen

148

Afrasiab's cities only, Samarcand,
Bokhara, and lone Khiva in the waste,   760
And the black Toorkmun tents; and only drunk
The desert rivers, Moorghab and Tejend,
Kohik, and where the Kalmucks feed their sheep,
The northern Sir; and this great Oxus stream,
The yellow Oxus, by whose brink I die.'
  Then, with a heavy groan, Rustum bewailed:–
'Oh, that its waves were flowing over me!
Oh, that I saw its grains of yellow silt
Roll tumbling in the current o'er my head!'
  But, with a grave mild voice, Sohrab replied:–   770
'Desire not that, my father! thou must live.
For some are born to do great deeds, and live,
As some are born to be obscured, and die.
Do thou the deeds I die too young to do,
And reap a second glory in thine age;
Thou art my father, and thy gain is mine.
But come! thou seest this great host of men
Which follow me; I pray thee, slay not these!
Let me entreat for them; what have they done?
They followed me, my hope, my fame, my star.   780
Let them all cross the Oxus back in peace.
But me thou must bear hence, not send with them,
But carry me with thee to Seistan,
And place me on a bed, and mourn for me,
Thou, and the snow-haired Zal, and all thy friends.
And thou must lay me in that lovely earth,
And heap a stately mound above my bones,
And plant a far-seen pillar over all.
That so the passing horseman on the waste
May see my tomb a great way off, and cry: 790
Sohrab, the mighty Rustum's son, lies there,
Whom his great father did in ignorance kill!
And I be not forgotten in my grave.'
  And, with a mournful voice, Rustum replied:–
'Fear not! as thou hast said, Sohrab, my son,

149

So shall it be; for I will burn my tents,
And quit the host, and bear thee hence with me,
And carry thee away to Seistan,
And place thee on a bed, and mourn for thee,
With the snow-headed Zal, and all my friends.   800
And I will lay thee in that lovely earth,
And heap a stately mound above thy bones,
And plant a far-seen pillar over all,
And men shall not forget thee in thy grave.
And I will spare thy host; yea, let them go!
Let them all cross the Oxus back in peace!
What should I do with slaying any more?
For would that all whom I have ever slain
Might be once more alive; my bitterest foes,
And they who were called champions in their time,   810
And through whose death I won that fame I have –
And I were nothing but a common man,
A poor, mean soldier, and without renown,
So thou mightest live too, my son, my son!
Or rather would that I, even I myself,
Might now be lying on this bloody sand,
Near death, and by an ignorant stroke of thine,
Not thou of mine! and I might die, not thou;
And I, not thou, be borne to Seistan;
And Zal might weep above my grave, not thine;   820
And say: *O son, I weep thee not too sore,*
For willingly, I know, thou met'st thine end!
But now in blood and battles was my youth,
And full of blood and battles is my age,
And I shall never end this life of blood.'
  Then, at the point of death, Sohrab replied:–
'A life of blood indeed, thou dreadful man!
But thou shalt yet have peace; only not now,
Not yet! but thou shalt have it on that day,
When thou shalt sail in a high-masted ship,   830
Thou and the other peers of Kai Khosroo,
Returning home over the salt blue sea,

From laying thy dear master in his grave.'

And Rustum gazed in Sohrab's face, and said:–
'Soon be that day, my son, and deep that sea!
Till then, if fate so wills, let me endure.'

He spoke; and Sohrab smiled on him, and took
The spear, and drew it from his side, and eased
His wound's imperious anguish; but the blood
Came welling from the open gash, and life   840
Flowed with the stream; all down his cold white side
The crimson torrent ran, dim now and soiled,
Like the soiled tissue of white violets
Left, freshly gathered, on their native bank,
By children whom their nurses call with haste
Indoors from the sun's eye; his head drooped low,
His limbs grew slack; motionless, white, he lay –
White, with eyes closed; only when heavy gasps,
Deep heavy gasps quivering through all his frame,
Convulsed him back to life, he opened them,   850
And fixed them feebly on his father's face;
Till now all strength was ebbed, and from his limbs
Unwillingly the spirit fled away,
Regretting the warm mansion which it left,
And youth, and bloom, and this delightful world.

So, on the bloody sand, Sohrab lay dead;
And the great Rustum drew his horseman's cloak
Down o'er his face, and sate by his dead son.
As those black granite pillars, once high-reared
By Jemshid in Persepolis, to bear   860
His house, now 'mid their broken flights of steps
Lie prone, enormous, down the mountain side –
So in the sand lay Rustum by his son.

And night came down over the solemn waste,
And the two gazing hosts, and that sole pair,
And darkened all; and a cold fog, with night,
Crept from the Oxus. Soon a hum arose,
As of a great assembly loosed, and fires
Began to twinkle through the fog; for now

Both armies moved to camp, and took their meal;   870
The Persians took it on the open sands
Southward, the Tartars by the river marge;
And Rustum and his son were left alone.
   But the majestic river floated on,
Out of the mist and hum of that low land,
Into the frosty starlight, and there moved,
Rejoicing, through the hushed Chorasmian waste,
Under the solitary moon; he flowed
Right for the polar star, past Orgunjè,
Brimming, and bright, and large; then sands begin   880
To hem his watery march, and dam his streams,
And split his currents; that for many a league
The shorn and parcelled Oxus strains along
Through beds of sand and matted rushy isles –
Oxus, forgetting the bright speed he had
In his high mountain-cradle in Pamere,
A foiled circuitous wanderer – till at last
The longed-for dash of waves is heard, and wide
His luminous home of waters opens, bright
And tranquil, from whose floor the new-bathed stars   890
Emerge, and shine upon the Aral Sea.

The Scholar-Gipsy

Go, for they call you, shepherd, from the hill;
   Go, shepherd, and untie the wattled cotes!
      No longer leave thy wistful flock unfed,
   Nor let thy bawling fellows rack their throats,
   Nor the cropped herbage shoot another head.
      But when the fields are still,
And the tired men and dogs all gone to rest,
   And only the white sheep are sometimes seen
   Cross and recross the strips of moon-blanched green,
Come, shepherd, and again begin the quest!   10

Here, where the reaper was at work of late –
    In this high field's dark corner, where he leaves
        His coat, his basket, and his earthen cruse,
    And in the sun all morning binds the sheaves,
        Then here, at noon, comes back his stores to use –
            Here will I sit and wait,
    While to my ear from uplands far away
        The bleating of the folded flocks is borne,
        With distant cries of reapers in the corn –
    All the live murmur of a summer's day.   20

Screened is this nook o'er the high, half-reaped field,
    And here till sun-down, shepherd! will I be.
        Through the thick corn the scarlet poppies peep,
        And round green roots and yellowing stalks I see
            Pale pink convolvulus in tendrils creep;
                And air-swept lindens yield
        Their scent, and rustle down their perfumed showers
            Of bloom on the bent grass where I am laid,
            And bower me from the August sun with shade;
        And the eye travels down to Oxford's towers.   30

And near me on the grass lies Glanvil's book –
    Come, let me read the oft-read tale again!
        The story of the Oxford scholar poor,
    Of pregnant parts and quick inventive brain,
        Who, tired of knocking at preferment's door,
            One summer-morn forsook
        His friends, and went to learn the gipsy-lore,
            And roamed the world with that wild brotherhood,
            And came, as most men deemed, to little good,
        But came to Oxford and his friends no more.   40

But once, years after, in the country-lanes,
    Two scholars, whom at college erst he knew,
        Met him, and of his way of life enquired;
    Whereat he answered, that the gipsy-crew,

His mates, had arts to rule as they desired
    The workings of men's brains,
And they can bind them to what thoughts they will.
    'And I,' he said, 'the secret of their art,
    When fully learned, will to the world impart;
But it needs heaven-sent moments for this skill.'   50

This said, he left them, and returned no more.
    But rumours hung about the country-side,
      That the lost Scholar long was seen to stray,
    Seen by rare glimpses, pensive and tongue-tied,
      In hat of antique shape, and cloak of grey,
        The same the gipsies wore.
Shepherds had met him on the Hurst in spring;
    At some lone alehouse in the Berkshire moors,
      On the warm ingle-bench, the smock-frocked boors
Had found him seated at their entering,   60

But, 'mid their drink and clatter, he would fly.
    And I myself seem half to know thy looks,
      And put the shepherds, wanderer! on thy trace;
    And boys who in lone wheatfields scare the rooks
      I ask if thou hast passed their quiet place;
        Or in my boat I lie
Moored to the cool bank in the summer-heats,
    'Mid wide grass meadows which the sunshine fills,
    And watch the warm, green-muffled Cumner hills,
And wonder if thou haunt'st their shy retreats.   70

For most, I know, thou lov'st retiréd ground!
    Thee at the ferry Oxford riders blithe,
      Returning home on summer-nights, have met
Crossing the stripling Thames at Bab-lock-hithe,
    Trailing in the cool stream thy fingers wet,
      As the punt's rope chops round;
And leaning backward in a pensive dream,
    And fostering in thy lap a heap of flowers

Plucked in shy fields and distant Wychwood bowers,
    And thine eyes resting on the moonlit stream.   80

And then they land, and thou art seen no more!
    Maidens, who from the distant hamlets come
        To dance around the Fyfield elm in May,
    Oft through the darkening fields have seen thee roam,
        Or cross a stile into the public way.
            Oft thou hast given them store
    Of flowers – the frail-leafed, white anemone,
        Dark bluebells drenched with dews of summer eves,
        And purple orchises with spotted leaves –
    But none hath words she can report of thee.   90

And, above Godstow Bridge, when hay-time's here
    In June, and many a scythe in sunshine flames,
        Men who through those wide fields of breezy grass
    Where black-winged swallows haunt the glittering Thames,
        To bathe in the abandoned lasher pass,
            Have often passed thee near
    Sitting upon the river bank o'ergrown;
        Marked thine outlandish garb, thy figure spare,
        Thy dark vague eyes, and soft abstracted air –
    But, when they came from bathing, thou wast gone!   100

At some lone homestead in the Cumner hills,
    Where at her open door the housewife darns,
        Thou hast been seen, or hanging on a gate
    To watch the threshers in the mossy barns.
        Children, who early range these slopes and late
            For cresses from the rills,
    Have known thee eying, all an April-day,
        The springing pastures and the feeding kine;
        And marked thee, when the stars come out and shine,
    Through the long dewy grass move slow away.   110

In autumn, on the skirts of Bagley Wood –
   Where most the gipsies by the turf-edged way
     Pitch their smoked tents, and every bush you see
   With scarlet patches tagged and shreds of grey,
     Above the forest-ground called Thessaly –
       The blackbird, picking food,
   Sees thee, nor stops his meal, nor fears at all;
     So often has he known thee past him stray,
     Rapt, twirling in thy hand a withered spray,
   And waiting for the spark from heaven to fall.   120

And once, in winter, on the causeway chill
   Where home through flooded fields foot-travellers go,
     Have I not passed thee on the wooden bridge,
   Wrapped in thy cloak and battling with the snow,
     Thy face tow'rd Hinksey and its wintry ridge?
       And thou hast climbed the hill,
   And gained the white brow of the Cumner range;
     Turned once to watch, while thick the snowflakes fall,
     The line of festal light in Christ-Church hall –
   Then sought thy straw in some sequestered grange.   130

But what – I dream! Two hundred years are flown
   Since first thy story ran through Oxford halls,
     And the grave Glanvil did the tale inscribe
   That thou wert wandered from the studious walls
     To learn strange arts, and join a gipsy-tribe;
       And thou from earth art gone
   Long since, and in some quiet churchyard laid –
     Some country-nook, where o'er thy unknown grave
     Tall grasses and white flowering nettles wave,
   Under a dark, red-fruited yew-tree's shade.   140

– No, no, thou hast not felt the lapse of hours!
   For what wears out the life of mortal men?
     'Tis that from change to change their being rolls;
     'Tis that repeated shocks, again, again,

Exhaust the energy of strongest souls
  And numb the elastic powers.
Till having used our nerves with bliss and teen,
  And tired upon a thousand schemes our wit,
  To the just-pausing Genius we remit
Our worn-out life, and are – what we have been.   150

Thou hast not lived, why should'st thou perish, so?
  Thou hadst *one* aim, *one* business, *one* desire;
    Else wert thou long since numbered with the dead!
  Else hadst thou spent, like other men, thy fire!
    The generations of thy peers are fled,
      And we ourselves shall go;
  But thou possessest an immortal lot,
    And we imagine thee exempt from age
    And living as thou liv'st on Glanvil's page,
  Because thou hadst – what we, alas! have not.   160

For early didst thou leave the world, with powers
  Fresh, undiverted to the world without,
    Firm to their mark, not spent on other things;
  Free from the sick fatigue, the languid doubt,
    Which much to have tried, in much been baffled, brings.
      O life unlike to ours!
  Who fluctuate idly without term or scope,
    Of whom each strives, nor knows for what he strives,
    And each half-lives a hundred different lives;
  Who wait like thee, but not, like thee, in hope.   170

Thou waitest for the spark from heaven! and we,
  Light half-believers of our casual creeds,
    Who never deeply felt, nor clearly willed,
  Whose insight never has borne fruit in deeds,
    Whose vague resolves never have been fulfilled;
      For whom each year we see
  Breeds new beginnings, disappointments new;
    Who hesitate and falter life away,

157

And lose to-morrow the ground won to-day –
Ah! do not we, wanderer! await it too?   180

Yes, we await it! – but it still delays,
    And then we suffer! and amongst us one,
        Who most has suffered, takes dejectedly
    His seat upon the intellectual throne;
        And all his store of sad experience he
            Lays bare of wretched days;
    Tells us his misery's birth and growth and signs,
        And how the dying spark of hope was fed,
        And how the breast was soothed, and how the head,
    And all his hourly varied anodynes.   190

This for our wisest! and we others pine,
    And wish the long unhappy dream would end,
        And waive all claim to bliss, and try to bear;
    With close-lipped patience for our only friend,
        Sad patience, too near neighbour to despair –
            But none has hope like thine!
    Thou through the fields and through the woods dost stray,
        Roaming the country-side, a truant boy,
        Nursing thy project in unclouded joy,
    And every doubt long blown by time away.   200

O born in days when wits were fresh and clear,
    And life ran gaily as the sparkling Thames;
        Before this strange disease of modern life,
    With its sick hurry, its divided aims,
        Its heads o'ertaxed, its palsied hearts, was rife –
            Fly hence, our contact fear!
    Still fly, plunge deeper in the bowering wood!
        Averse, as Dido did with gesture stern
        From her false friend's approach in Hades turn,
    Wave us away, and keep thy solitude!   210

158

Still nursing the unconquerable hope,
　　Still clutching the inviolable shade,
　　　With a free, onward impulse brushing through,
　　By night, the silvered branches of the glade –
　　　Far on the forest-skirts, where none pursue,
　　　　On some mild pastoral slope
　　Emerge, and resting on the moonlit pales
　　　Freshen thy flowers as in former years
　　　With dew, or listen with enchanted ears,
　　From the dark dingles, to the nightingales!　　　　　220

But fly our paths, our feverish contact fly!
　　For strong the infection of our mental strife,
　　　Which, though it gives no bliss, yet spoils for rest;
　　And we should win thee from thy own fair life,
　　　Like us distracted, and like us unblest.
　　　　Soon, soon thy cheer would die,
　　Thy hopes grow timorous, and unfixed thy powers,
　　　And thy clear aims be cross and shifting made;
　　　And then thy glad perennial youth would fade,
　　Fade, and grow old at last, and die like ours.　　　　230

Then fly our greetings, fly our speech and smiles!
　　– As some grave Tyrian trader, from the sea,
　　　Descried at sunrise an emerging prow
　　Lifting the cool-haired creepers stealthily,
　　　The fringes of a southward-facing brow
　　　　Among the Ægean isles;
　　And saw the merry Grecian coaster come,
　　　Freighted with amber grapes, and Chian wine,
　　　Green, bursting figs, and tunnies steeped in brine –
　　And knew the intruders on his ancient home,　　　　240

The young light-hearted masters of the waves –
　　And snatched his rudder, and shook out more sail;
　　　And day and night held on indignantly
　　O'er the blue Midland waters with the gale,

Betwixt the Syrtes and soft Sicily,
    To where the Atlantic raves
Outside the western straits; and unbent sails
    There, where down cloudy cliffs, through sheets of foam,
    Shy traffickers, the dark Iberians come;
And on the beach undid his corded bales.   250

Requiescat

Strew on her roses, roses,
    And never a spray of yew!
In quiet she reposes;
    Ah, would that I did too!

Her mirth the world required;
    She bathed it in smiles of glee.
But her heart was tired, tired,
    And now they let her be.

Her life was turning, turning,
    In mazes of heat and sound.
But for peace her soul was yearning,
    And now peace laps her round.

Her cabined, ample spirit,
    It fluttered and failed for breath.
To-night it doth inherit
    The vasty hall of death.

Thyrsis

A MONODY, *to commemorate the author's friend,*
ARTHUR HUGH CLOUGH, *who died at Florence, 1861*

How changed is here each spot man makes or fills!
  In the two Hinkseys nothing keeps the same;
    The village street its haunted mansion lacks,
  And from the sign is gone Sibylla's name,
    And from the roofs the twisted chimney-stacks –
      Are ye too changed, ye hills?
  See, 'tis no foot of unfamiliar men
    To-night from Oxford up your pathway strays!
    Here came I often, often, in old days –
  Thyrsis and I; we still had Thyrsis then.   10

Runs it not here, the track by Childsworth Farm,
  Past the high wood, to where the elm-tree crowns
    The hill behind whose ridge the sunset flames?
  The signal-elm, that looks on Ilsley Downs,
    The Vale, the three lone weirs, the youthful Thames?
      This winter-eve is warm,
  Humid the air! leafless, yet soft as spring,
    The tender purple spray on copse and briers!
    And that sweet city with her dreaming spires,
  She needs not June for beauty's heightening,   20

Lovely all times she lies, lovely to-night! –
  Only, methinks, some loss of habit's power
    Befalls me wandering through this upland dim.
  Once passed I blindfold here, at any hour;
    Now seldom come I, since I came with him.
      That single elm-tree bright
  Against the west – I miss it! is it gone?
    We prized it dearly; while it stood, we said,
    Our friend, the Gipsy-Scholar, was not dead;
  While the tree lived, he in these fields lived on.   30

Too rare, too rare, grow now my visits here,
　　But once I knew each field, each flower, each stick;
　　　And with the country-folk acquaintance made
　　By barn in threshing time, by new-built rick.
　　　Here, too, our shepherd-pipes we first assayed.
　　　　Ah me! this many a year
　　My pipe is lost, my shepherd's holiday!
　　　Needs must I lose them, needs with heavy heart
　　　Into the world and wave of men depart;
　　But Thyrsis of his own will went away.　　　　　　　40

It irked him to be here, he could not rest.
　　He loved each simple joy the country yields,
　　　He loved his mates; but yet he could not keep,
　　For that a shadow loured on the fields,
　　　Here with the shepherds and the silly sheep.
　　　　Some life of men unblest
　　He knew, which made him droop, and filled his head.
　　　He went; his piping took a troubled sound
　　　Of storms that rage outside our happy ground;
　　He could not wait their passing, he is dead.　　　　50

So, some tempestuous morn in early June,
　　When the year's primal burst of bloom is o'er,
　　　Before the roses and the longest day –
　　When garden-walks and all the grassy floor
　　　With blossoms red and white of fallen May
　　　And chestnut-flowers are strewn –
　　So have I heard the cuckoo's parting cry,
　　　From the wet field, through the vexed garden-trees,
　　　Come with the volleying rain and tossing breeze:
　　The bloom is gone, and with the bloom go I!　　　　60

Too quick despairer, wherefore wilt thou go?
　　Soon will the high Midsummer pomps come on,
　　　Soon will the musk carnations break and swell,
　　Soon shall we have gold-dusted snapdragon,

Sweet-William with his homely cottage-smell,
   And stocks in fragrant blow;
Roses that down the alleys shine afar,
   And open, jasmine-muffled lattices,
   And groups under the dreaming garden-trees,
And the full moon, and the white evening-star.   70

He hearkens not! light comer, he is flown!
   What matters it? next year he will return,
   And we shall have him in the sweet spring-days,
   With whitening hedges, and uncrumpling fern,
   And blue-bells trembling by the forest-ways,
   And scent of hay new-mown.
But Thyrsis never more we swains shall see;
   See him come back, and cut a smoother reed,
   And blow a strain the world at last shall heed –
For Time, not Corydon, hath conquered thee!   80

Alack, for Corydon no rival now!
   But when Sicilian shepherds lost a mate,
   Some good survivor with his flute would go,
Piping a ditty sad for Bion's fate;
   And cross the unpermitted ferry's flow,
   And relax Pluto's brow,
And make leap up with joy the beauteous head
   Of Proserpine, among whose crownéd hair
   Are flowers first opened on Sicilian air,
And flute his friend, like Orpheus, from the dead.   90

O easy access to the hearer's grace
   When Dorian shepherds sang to Proserpine!
   For she herself had trod Sicilian fields,
She knew the Dorian water's gush divine,
   She knew each lily white which Enna yields,
   Each rose with blushing face;
She loved the Dorian pipe, the Dorian strain.
   But ah, of our poor Thames she never heard!

Her foot the Cumner cowslips never stirred;
   And we should tease her with our plaint in vain!   100

Well! wind-dispersed and vain the words will be,
   Yet, Thyrsis, let me give my grief its hour
      In the old haunt, and find our tree-topped hill!
   Who, if not I, for questing here hath power?
      I know the wood which hides the daffodil,
         I know the Fyfield tree,
   I know what white, what purple fritillaries
      The grassy harvest of the river-fields,
      Above by Ensham, down by Sandford, yields,
   And what sedged brooks are Thames's tributaries;   110

I know these slopes; who knows them if not I?
   But many a dingle on the loved hill-side,
      With thorns once studded, old, white-blossomed trees,
   Where thick the cowslips grew, and far descried
      High towered the spikes of purple orchises,
         Hath since our day put by
   The coronals of that forgotten time;
      Down each green bank hath gone the ploughboy's team,
      And only in the hidden brookside gleam
   Primroses, orphans of the flowery prime.   120

Where is the girl, who by the boatman's door,
   Above the locks, above the boating throng,
      Unmoored our skiff when through the Wytham flats,
   Red loosestrife and blond meadow-sweet among
      And darting swallows and light water-gnats,
         We tracked the shy Thames shore?
   Where are the mowers, who, as the tiny swell
      Of our boat passing heaved the river-grass,
      Stood with suspended scythe to see us pass?
   They all are gone, and thou art gone as well!   130

Yes, thou art gone! and round me too the night
　　In ever-nearing circle weaves her shade.
　　　　I see her veil draw soft across the day,
　　I feel her slowly chilling breath invade
　　　　The cheek grown thin, the brown hair sprent with grey;
　　　　　　I feel his finger light
　　Laid pausefully upon life's headlong train;
　　　　The foot less prompt to meet the morning dew,
　　　　The heart less bounding at emotion new,
　　And hope, once crushed, less quick to spring again.　　140

And long the way appears, which seemed so short
　　To the less practised eye of sanguine youth;
　　　　And high the mountain-tops, in cloudy air,
　　The mountain-tops where is the throne of Truth,
　　　　Tops in life's morning-sun so bright and bare!
　　　　　　Unbreachable the fort
　　Of the long-battered world uplifts its wall;
　　　　And strange and vain the earthly turmoil grows,
　　　　And near and real the charm of thy repose,
　　And night as welcome as a friend would fall.　　150

But hush! the upland hath a sudden loss
　　Of quiet! – Look, adown the dusk hill-side,
　　　　A troop of Oxford hunters going home,
　　As in old days, jovial and talking, ride!
　　　　From hunting with the Berkshire hounds they come.
　　　　　　Quick! let me fly, and cross
　　Into yon farther field! – 'Tis done; and see,
　　　　Backed by the sunset, which doth glorify
　　　　The orange and pale violet evening-sky,
　　Bare on its lonely ridge, the Tree! the Tree!　　160

I take the omen! Eve lets down her veil,
　　The white fog creeps from bush to bush about,
　　　　The west unflushes, the high stars grow bright,
　　And in the scattered farms the lights come out.

I cannot reach the signal-tree to-night,
    Yet, happy omen, hail!
Hear it from thy broad lucent Arno-vale
    (For there thine earth-forgetting eyelids keep
    The morningless and unawakening sleep
Under the flowery oleanders pale),   170

Hear it, O Thyrsis, still our tree is there!
    Ah, vain! These English fields, this upland dim,
    These brambles pale with mist engarlanded,
That lone, sky-pointing tree, are not for him;
    To a boon southern country he is fled,
        And now in happier air,
Wandering with the great Mother's train divine
    (And purer or more subtle soul than thee,
    I trow, the mighty Mother doth not see)
Within a folding of the Apennine,   180

Thou hearest the immortal chants of old!
    Putting his sickle to the perilous grain
    In the hot cornfield of the Phrygian king,
For thee the Lityerses-song again
    Young Daphnis with his silver voice doth sing;
        Sings his Sicilian fold,
His sheep, his hapless love, his blinded eyes –
    And how a call celestial round him rang,
    And heavenward from the fountain-brink he sprang,
And all the marvel of the golden skies.   190

There thou art gone, and me thou leavest here
    Sole in these fields! yet will I not despair.
    Despair I will not, while I yet descry
'Neath the mild canopy of English air
    That lonely tree against the western sky.
        Still, still these slopes, 'tis clear,
Our Gipsy-Scholar haunts, outliving thee!
    Fields where soft sheep from cages pull the hay,

Woods with anemones in flower till May,
Know him a wanderer still; then why not me?   200

A fugitive and gracious light he seeks,
  Shy to illumine; and I seek it too.
    This does not come with houses or with gold,
  With place, with honour, and a flattering crew;
    'Tis not in the world's market bought and sold –
      But the smooth-slipping weeks
  Drop by, and leave its seeker still untired;
    Out of the heed of mortals he is gone,
    He wends unfollowed, he must house alone;
  Yet on he fares, by his own heart inspired.   210

Thou too, O Thyrsis, on like quest wast bound;
  Thou wanderedst with me for a little hour!
    Men gave thee nothing; but this happy quest,
  If men esteemed thee feeble, gave thee power,
    If men procured thee trouble, gave thee rest.
      And this rude Cumner ground,
  Its fir-topped Hurst, its farms, its quiet fields,
    Here cam'st thou in thy jocund youthful time,
    Here was thine height of strength, thy golden prime!
  And still the haunt beloved a virtue yields.   220

What though the music of thy rustic flute
  Kept not for long its happy, country tone;
    Lost it too soon, and learnt a stormy note
  Of men contention-tossed, of men who groan,
    Which tasked thy pipe too sore, and tired thy throat
      It failed, and thou wast mute!
  Yet hadst thou alway visions of our light,
    And long with men of care thou couldst not stay,
    And soon thy foot resumed its wandering way,
  Left human haunt, and on alone till night.   230

167

Too rare, too rare, grow now my visits here!
   'Mid city-noise, not, as with thee of yore,
     Thyrsis! in reach of sheep-bells is my home.
   – Then through the great town's harsh, heart-wearying roar,
     Let in thy voice a whisper often come,
       To chase fatigue and fear:
Why faintest thou? I wandered till I died.
   Roam on! The light we sought is shining still.
    Dost thou ask proof? Our tree yet crowns the hill,
Our Scholar travels yet the loved hill-side.   240

Growing Old

What is it to grow old?
Is it to lose the glory of the form,
The lustre of the eye?
Is it for beauty to forgo her wreath?
– Yes, but not this alone.

Is it to feel our strength –
Not our bloom only, but our strength – decay?
Is it to feel each limb
Grow stiffer, every function less exact,
Each nerve more loosely strung?   10

Yes, this, and more; but not
Ah, 'tis not what in youth we dreamed 'twould be!
'Tis not to have our life
Mellowed and softened as with sunset-glow,
A golden day's decline.

'Tis not to see the world
As from a height, with rapt prophetic eyes,
And heart profoundly stirred;
And weep, and feel the fullness of the past,
The years that are no more.   20

It is to spend long days
And not once feel that we were ever young;
It is to add, immured
In the hot prison of the present, month
To month with weary pain.

It is to suffer this,
And feel but half, and feebly, what we feel.
Deep in our hidden heart
Festers the dull remembrance of a change,
But no emotion – none.   30

It is – last stage of all –
When we are frozen up within, and quite
The phantom of ourselves,
To hear the world applaud the hollow ghost
Which blamed the living man.

The Last Word

Creep into thy narrow bed,
Creep, and let no more be said!
Vain thy onset! all stands fast.
Thou thyself must break at last.

Let the long contention cease!
Geese are swans, and swans are geese.
Let them have it how they will!
Thou art tired; best be still.

They out-talked thee, hissed thee, tore thee?
Better men fared thus before thee;
Fired their ringing shot and passed,
Hotly charged – and sank at last.

Charge once more, then, and be dumb!
Let the victors, when they come,
When the forts of folly fall,
Find thy body by the wall!

Index of first lines

Border Ballads: a selection
edited by James Reid

Poetry by English Women:
Elizabethan to Victorian
edited by R.E. Pritchard

The Poorhouse Fugitives:
Self-taught poets & poetry in
Victorian Britain
edited by Brian Maidment

AKENSIDE, MACPHERSON & YOUNG
Selected Poetry
edited by S.H. Clark

MATTHEW ARNOLD (1822-1888)
Selected Poems
edited by Keith Silver

WILLIAM BARNES (1801-1886)
Selected Poems
edited by Robert Nye

APHRA BEHN (1640-1689)
Selected Poems
edited by Malcolm Hicks

THOMAS BEWICK (1753-1828)
Selected Work
edited by Robyn Marsack

EDMUND BLUNDEN (1896-1974)
Selected Poems
edited by Robyn Marsack

THE BRONTË SISTERS
Selected Poems of Charlotte,
Emily and Anne Brontë
edited by Stevie Davies

ELIZABETH BARRETT BROWNING
(1806-1861)
Selected Poems
edited by Malcolm Hicks

THOMAS CAMPION (1752-1770)
Ayres and Observations
edited by Joan Hart

THOMAS CHATTERTON (1752-1770)
Selected Poems
edited by Grevel Lindop

JOHN CLARE (1793-1864)
The Midsummer Cushion
edited by R.K.R. Thornton
& Anne Tibble

Cottage Tales
edited by Eric Robinson, David
Powell & P.M.S. Dawson

ARTHUR HUGH CLOUGH (1819-1861)
Selected Poems
edited by Shirley Chew

SAMUEL TAYLOR COLERIDGE
(1772-1834)
Selected Poetry
edited by William Empson
& David Pirie

173

ANDREW MARVELL (1621-1678)
Selected Poems
edited by Bill Hutchings

JOHN MASEFIELD (1878-1967)
Selected Poems
edited by Donald Stanford

GEORGE MEREDITH (1828-1909)
Selected Poems
edited by Keith Hanley

WILLIAM MORRIS (1834-1896)
Selected Poems
edited by Peter Faulkner

JOHN WILMOT, EARL OF ROCHESTER
(1648-1680)
The Debt to Pleasure
edited by John Adlard

CHRISTINA ROSSETTI (1830-1894)
Selected Poems
edited by C.H. Sisson

DANTE GABRIEL ROSSETTI (1828-1892)
Selected Poems and Translations
edited by Clive Wilmer

SIR WALTER SCOTT (1771-1832)
Selected Poems
edited by James Reed

MARY SIDNEY, COUNTESS OF
PEMBROKE (1561-1621)
& SIR PHILIP SIDNEY
The Sidney Psalms
edited by R.E. Pritchard

SIR PHILIP SIDNEY (1554-1586)
Selected Writings
edited by Richard Dutton

JOHN SKELTON (1460-1529)
Selected Poems
edited by Gerald Hammond

CHRISTOPHER SMART (1722-1771)
The Religious Poetry
edited by Marcus Walsh

HENRY HOWARD, EARL OF SURREY
(1517-1547)
Selected Poems
edited by Dennis Keene

JONATHAN SWIFT (1667-1745)
Selected Poems
edited by C.H. Sisson

ALGERNON CHARLES SWINBURNE
(1837-1909)
Selected Poems
edited by L.M. Findlay

ARTHUR SYMONS (1865-1945)
Selected Writings
edited by R.V. Holdsworth

JEREMY TAYLOR (1613-1667)
Selected Writings
edited by C.H. Sisson

THOMAS TRAHERNE (1637?-1674)
Selected Writings
edited by Dick Davis

HENRY VAUGHAN (1622-1695)
Selected Poems
edited by Robert B. Shaw

OSCAR WILDE (1854-1900)
Selected Poems
edited by Malcolm Hicks